PROPHETIC DESTINY 101

A Daily Guide of Prophecy
and Prayer To Fulfill Your
God-Ordained Future

MICHAEL K. HURD

Prophetic Destiny 101
A Daily Guide of Prophecy and Prayer
To Fulfill Your God-Ordained Future
Michael K. Hurd

To contact the author:
Michael K. Hurd
Prophetic.destiny66@gmail.com

Published by:

Mary Ethel

Mary Ethel Eckard
Frisco, Texas

Library of Congress Control Number: 2026903422
ISBN (Print): 978-1-966561-37-8
ISBN (E-book): 978-1-966561-38-5

DEDICATION

This book is dedicated to all who are still incarcerated,
those behind physical bars, and those who feel
trapped in their minds and hearts.
May you come to know the love of Jesus as your Lord and Savior,
and may you realize that you are no longer a slave to your past.
In Him, you are truly free.

CONTENTS

I've walked a long journey with Mike Hurd through some of the worst times, as well as some of the best. The one part of that journey that sticks out in my mind more than any other is his desire to serve Jesus! That has never changed or even wavered! Even in the worst of circumstances and situations, through failures and triumphs, Mike's heart was to live a life pleasing to God.

I know the part of his life that I've been privileged to share has resulted in his commitment to study the Word, and it's out of that diligent study that have come the words of this book. Prophecy is one of those theological areas that is often confused as being merely a "foretelling of the future," and that certainly is a part of what prophecy is all about. There is, however, and it is evident in Mike's writing, the part of prophecy that is much more a speaking forth the Word of God, and that is what Mike has done over the majority of his journey with Christ.

Even in the most difficult of circumstances, and in what I'm sure were the most difficult for him to navigate, Mike's commitment to "hide the Word in his heart" was very evident. I can recall numerous times when he faced what seemed to be insurmountable obstacles that could and often did throw him "off track," but he would simply recall from memory the Word that God had planted in his heart, which allowed him to get back "on track!"

I can honestly say there are very few people in this world who have brought a greater degree of the godly kind of pride to my life more than Mike. We have prayed together, I'm certain there were times when we cried together, and many times when we could only smile at whatever the devil was trying to come against us, from being told we couldn't worship in certain places to dealing with those who didn't want to extend grace as Jesus would! We smiled because, if we didn't, our hearts would break! But through it all, Mike was an encouragement to me because he had personally encountered and overcome much larger obstacles than those I had ever faced, as well as those we faced together.

It's for these reasons and many more that I feel so honored and privileged to be able to recommend "Prophetic Destiny 101!"

Terence (Terry) D. Engler
Booker Christian Church
Booker, Texas

This is no ordinary devotional; it is one that parallels real-life experiences and testimonies to the trials and tribulations of Michael Hurd.

I had the opportunity to meet Mr. Hurd at the house of Joshua in Topeka, Kansas. He eventually joined Increase Your Faith In Christ Temple Of Deliverance. While attending, Michael served in any capacity asked of him, and his level of commitment was a testament to his love and devotion for God and others.

Michaels' love for the Word of God is apparent as is his love for the broken-hearted. He has a testimony that would test the limits of any of us. He is a man of God, standing for truth and righteousness. I watched him fight to overcome serious obstacles! He recognizes God's authority and lives in submission to it, accepting God's instructions and carrying them out with joy.

He is not self-centered but lives to love and serve others, putting their needs before his own. This includes being a servant-leader and serving the community. Michael maintains a deep personal communion with God, who is using him to serve those who are displaced, homeless, and broken! His testimony is not one without trials and tribulations! I have watched him grow and develop his gifts while also witnessing his personal deliverance.

This devotional was divinely inspired. As you find yourself in each page, you will encounter the grand programmer of the world, Jesus Christ. I hope this encourages, delivers, and brings hope to you, and propels you into the work of love and forgiveness of the Savior, our Lord Jesus Christ.

Pastor Tracy C. Smith
Increase Your Faith in Christ Temple of Deliverance
Topeka, Kansas

INTRODUCTION

When you read the Bible, do you ever notice how the lives of the people in Scripture can sometimes mirror your own? The story of King Jehoiachin has always reminded me a lot of myself.

> *"Jehoiachin was only eighteen years old when he became king, and he reigned a short three months. Scripture says he "did evil in the eyes of the Lord," following the same pattern as his father. Eventually, Nebuchadnezzar took him captive to Babylon along with his family and leaders."*
> 2 Kings 24:8-9, 15

> *"But then, after thirty-seven years in captivity, something incredible happened. The new king of Babylon released Jehoiachin from prison, spoke kindly to him, and even gave him a seat of honor above all the other captive kings. Jehoiachin took off his prison clothes, set them aside and, for the rest of his life, ate daily at the king's table."*
> 2 Kings 25:27-29

I, too, was incarcerated at the age of eighteen and, just like him, when I was released, I set aside my prison clothes, physically and spiritually, and God welcomed me to His table. Connecting my story with the story of Jehoiachin helped me see the Word of God in a deeper, more personal way.

I continue to pray for those who are still incarcerated. For their freedom from oppression, for God's peace to guard their minds, and for the hope to never fade from their hearts.

As I've had the privilege of sharing my testimony, the image of Jehoiachin being released from prison and then being invited to "eat regularly at the king's table" continues to move me. It is a beautiful picture of restoration and favor, of God's righteous judgment *and* His merciful grace.

Lord, I thank You for being the God who frees, restores, and lifts us into places we never imagined we could stand. Just as You brought Jehoiachin out of captivity and set him at the king's table, You have brought me out of my own bondage and invited me into fellowship with You.

Father, I lift every person who is still incarcerated, those physically behind walls and those spiritually bound by guilt, fear, or hopelessness. Let Your peace guard their hearts. Let Your light break through their darkness. Remind them that no prison, no past, and no mistake is greater than Your grace.

Holy Spirit, continue to shape my life into a testimony of Your mercy. Help me walk in humility, obedience, and boldness, always remembering where You brought me from, and always pointing others to the One who sets captives free.

Thank You, Lord, for letting me dine at Your table. May my life honor You always. In Jesus' name. Amen.

YOU ARE A TEMPLE OF GOD

Salvation occurred the moment you believed that Christ's work on the cross was complete, and that should never be questioned. Jesus gave His all, paying for the sins of the entire world. In return, He desires all of you.

God has a unique calling for your life, and He has a purpose designed specifically for you. You cannot outsmart God's plan. Even when we look at the story of Eli and his sons' disobedience, we see that God still has a purpose, no matter what. Just as He gave Eli and his sons a calling, He has called you too.

The scripture says, *"Then the Lord called Samuel."*

God places people in your life to help bring His purpose into reality. When God calls, it's important to respond just as Samuel did: *"'Here I am.' And he ran to Eli and said, 'Here I am; you called me.'"*

God has surrounded you with people who are part of His plan, guiding you toward what He wants you to do. You were created for His glory and His service, and even if you resist or deny it, He will continue to use others to confirm His will for you.

How many times has God called, only for you to dismiss it as the words of others rather than His? Why didn't He just speak directly to you?

Maybe God has placed you under the care of someone to test your obedience to His direction through them. If you can't honor them, how can you expect to honor God? As Paul reminds us in 1 Timothy 5:17, we are to give "double honor" to those who preach and teach. When we show honor, it's not just the leader who is blessed—it blesses the entire church community.

Consider what happened when Samuel chose to listen and obey.

"The Lord called again, 'Samuel!' Samuel went to Eli once more, saying, 'Here I am; you called me.' But Eli replied, 'I did not call; go back and lie down.' Samuel did not yet know the Lord, and the word

*of the Lord had not been revealed to him. A third time the Lord called,
'Samuel!' Samuel again went to Eli and said, 'Here I am; you called
me.' Finally, Eli understood that the Lord was calling the boy. He told
Samuel, 'Go and lie down. If He calls you again, say, "Speak, Lord, for
your servant is listening."' So Samuel went back and lay down. Then
the Lord came and stood there, calling as before, 'Samuel! Samuel!'
And Samuel responded, 'Speak, for your servant is listening.'"*
1 Samuel 3:6-10

At that moment, God revealed His calling to Samuel. He shared a
prophecy about Israel and judgment on Eli's household.

*"See, I am about to do something in Israel that will make the ears of
everyone who hears it tingle. At that time, I will carry out against Eli
everything I spoke about his family, from beginning to end. I told him
I would judge his family forever because of the sin he knew about—his
sons blasphemed God, and he failed to stop them. Therefore, I swore that
the guilt of Eli's house will never be atoned for by sacrifice or offering."*
1 Samuel 3:11-14

THE GIFT OF OBEDIENCE

Partial obedience creates a false sense of faith, one that leads to consequences and restricts God's power in our lives.

God gives His favor upon those He has anointed. The Bible warns that in the last days, many within the faith will fall away.

We can't treat God's Word like a fast-food menu, picking and choosing what suits us with a "have it your way" mentality.

In fact, Scripture teaches us what happens when we follow God's Word and what truly pleases Him. Hebrews 11:6 tells us, *"And without faith, it is impossible to please him, for whoever would draw near to God must believe that he exists and that he rewards those who seek him."*

God's Word also commands us to remain faithful to His calling and protect it at all costs.

"Since you have kept my command to endure patiently, I will also keep you from the hour of trial that is going to come on the whole world to test the inhabitants of the earth. I am coming soon. Hold on to what you have, so that no one will take your crown. The one who is victorious I will make a pillar in the temple of my God. Never again will they leave it. I will write on them the name of my God and the name of the city of my God, the new Jerusalem, which is coming down out of heaven from my God; and I will also write on them my new name. He who has an ear, let him hear what the Spirit says to the churches."
Revelation 3:10-12

3

SET APART AND USED BY GOD

The moment we accept Christ, we are born again and the Holy Spirit gives us everything needed to be set apart and used by God.

This is the story of Samuel and how his mother, Hannah, offered him to the temple. That promise of God in those days is what set him apart.

"Once when they had finished eating and drinking in Shiloh, Hannah stood up. Now Eli the priest was sitting on his chair by the doorpost of the Lord's house. In her deep anguish Hannah prayed to the Lord, weeping bitterly. And she made a vow, saying, 'Lord Almighty, if you will only look on your servant's misery and remember me, and not forget your servant but give her a son, then I will give him to the Lord for all the days of his life, and no razor will ever be used on his head.' As she kept on praying to the Lord, Eli observed her mouth. Hannah was praying in her heart, and her lips were moving but her voice was not heard. Eli thought she was drunk."
1 Samuel 1:9-13

"For one who speaks in a tongue does not speak to men but to God, for no one understands, but in his spirit he speaks mysteries."
1 Corinthians 14:2

Look what Eli said to Hannah after she spoke in utterance to God.

"Then Eli said to her, 'How long will you behave like a drunk? Get rid of your wine!' But Hannah answered and said, 'No, my lord, I am a woman despairing in spirit; I have drunk neither wine nor strong drink, but I have poured out my soul before the Lord. Do not consider your bond-servant a useless woman, for I have spoken until now out of my great concern and provocation.' Then Eli answered and said, 'Go in peace; and may the God of Israel grant your request that you have asked of Him.'
1 Samuel 1:14-17

PRAISE IS YOUR WEAPON

A shepherd boy who played the lyre ministered to King Saul; his music opened the door to do warfare.

> *"And whenever the harmful spirit from God was upon Saul, David took the lyre and played it with his hand. So Saul was refreshed and was well, and the harmful spirit departed from him."*
> 1 Samuel 16:23

Praise is a weapon that Satan hates. He, before becoming an enemy to God, was the choir leader in the heavens. David quieted the evil spirits, but his music awoke the giants, and everyone was too afraid to fight them. David was sent by God to do the unthinkable.

> *"David asked the soldiers standing nearby, 'What will a man get for killing this Philistine and ending his defiance of Israel? Who is this pagan Philistine anyway, that he is allowed to defy the armies of the living God?' And these men gave David the same reply. They said, 'Yes, that is the reward for killing him.' But when David's oldest brother, Eliab, heard David talking to the men, he was angry. 'What are you doing around here anyway?' he demanded. 'What about those few sheep you're supposed to be taking care of? I know about your pride and deceit. You just want to see the battle!' 'What have I done now?' David replied. 'I was only asking a question!' He walked over to some others and asked them the same thing and received the same answer. Then David's question was reported to King Saul, and the king sent for him. 'Don't worry about this Philistine,' David told Saul. 'I'll go fight him!' 'Don't be ridiculous!' Saul replied. 'There's no way you can fight this Philistine and possibly win! You're only a boy, and he's been a man of war since his youth.'"*
> 1 Samuel 17:26-34

David knew who rescued him as he tells King Saul,

> *"'The LORD who rescued me from the claws of the lion and the bear*
> *will rescue me from this Philistine!' Saul finally consented.*
> *'All right, go ahead,' he said. 'And may the LORD be with you!'"*
> 1 Samuel 17:37

> *"Today the LORD will conquer you, and I will kill you and cut*
> *off your head. And then I will give the dead bodies of your men*
> *to the birds and wild animals, and the whole world will know*
> *that there is a God in Israel! And everyone assembled here will*
> *know that the LORD rescues his people, but not with sword and*
> *spear. This is the LORD's battle, and he will give you to us!"*
> 1 Samuel 17:46

When we decree and declare who God is, we can kill anything that opposes Him.

> *When the enemy shall come in like a flood,*
> *the Spirit of the LORD shall lift up a standard against him.*
> Isaiah 59:19

That standard is the name of Jesus.

> *"Behold, I give unto you power to tread on serpents and scorpions,*
> *and over all the power of the enemy: and nothing*
> *shall by any means hurt you."*
> Luke 10:19

Christ came to destroy the works of the Devil, and we are to take part in Christ's work as we expose the darkness with the truth of God's Word.

Prayer, Declare and Decree

Satan, we bind you in the name of Jesus, we rebuke you in Jesus' name.

We command you to leave our presence.

You are defeated by the blood of Jesus.

You have no power over us; by the stripes of Jesus we are healed.

We were bought with a price, with the blood of Jesus.

You have been defeated.

We proclaim and declare you are under our feet. We are the head and not the tail.

Get thee behind us.

We stand in the gap for the lost whose eyes have been blinded by your lies.

We claim victory for those who are held captive.

We lay hands on the sick and by our faith they are healed.

We bind up the wounds of the broken hearted and give hope to the hopeless.

We tear down all strongholds and cast out all evil spirits in the name of Jesus!

DAY

5

EVIL SPIRITS MUST FLEE

In Jesus' name, we do not war according to the flesh. For the weapons of our warfare are not carnal but mighty in God. They are for pulling down strongholds, casting down arguments and every high thing that exalts itself against the knowledge of God. They are for bringing every thought into captivity to the obedience of Christ.

I decree and declare God's Word; just as the spirit spoke to Abram, the Holy Spirit calls to me.

> *"When Abram heard that his relative had been taken*
> *captive, he called out the 318 trained men born in his*
> *household and went in pursuit as far as Dan."*
> Genesis 14:14

> *"For the word of God is living and active,*
> *sharper than any two-edged sword,*
> *piercing to the division of soul and of spirit, of joints and of marrow,*
> *and discerning the thoughts and intentions of the heart."*
> Hebrews 4:12

Out of the abundance of the heart the mouth speaks, and I decree and declare. Hear your servant cry, O God, shatter and shake free those that are held captive to addiction and those who are slaves to the lies of Satan.

> *"Let these false prophets tell their dreams, but let my true messengers*
> *faithfully proclaim my every word. There is a difference between*
> *straw and grain! 'Does not my word burn like fire?' says the Lord.*
> *'Is it not like a mighty hammer that smashes a rock to pieces?'"*
> Jeremiah 23:28-29

We decree and declare victory by the blood of Jesus; every evil spirit must flee in Jesus name!

DAY

6

TRANSFORMATION

Your offering to God is unique, set apart and established before the foundation of the world. Every step of faith you take has been predestined and ordained by God. The more you surrender, the more God works through you for His glory.

God takes what we see as worthless and transforms it into a vessel, humbled and broken before Him. We no longer desire to live by our own strength, but by the very power that raised our Lord Jesus from the grave!

"For if we are out of our mind, it is for God, or if we are of right mind,
it is for you. For the love of Christ controls us, having concluded this,
that one died for all, therefore all died. And He died for all,
so that they who live would no longer live for themselves,
but for Him who died and rose again on their behalf."
2 Corinthians 5:13-15

THE GOD WHO HEARS

When we feel we have been treated harshly, God sees us. Just as in Genesis 16, He saw Hagar, the maidservant who was given to Abram when Sarai could not conceive. In her distress, Hagar encountered an angel who spoke words of hope, telling her to return and submit to her mistress. Even in her fear and sadness, the Lord showed her that He had not abandoned her but was watching over her life.

> *"All of us who have had the veil removed can see and reflect*
> *the glory of the Lord. And the Lord, who is the Spirit,*
> *makes us more and more like him*
> *as we are changed into his glorious image."*
> 2 Corinthians 3:18

As all of us reflect the Lord's glory with faces that are not covered with veils, we are being changed into his image with ever-increasing glory. This comes from the Lord, who is the Spirit.

Lord Jesus, you take the broken and make it beautiful, you heal, mend, and restore lives.

We bless you and thank you for your goodness and grace.

You are the God who sees.

Open us, O Lord, to the predestined revelation Word of God.

Let us see into the heavenly realms.

Plant your vision deep within our spirit.

Loose and bind any hindering hesitation, any unbelief, or any unwavering hurt or regrets.

Start a flame within our hearts and burn up any rebellious attitudes, any vain or self-seeking motives or selfish ambition.

Impart to us what is needed to perform your will.

Place within us Your desires.

Forgive us of any knowing or unknowing sin or error that could hinder, wound, or obstruct Your divine interventions.

DAY

8

FUTURE GLORY

As I prayed and meditated on the following passages, I reflected on the transition that has taken place in the Church.

> *"'Behold, the days are coming,' says the Lord God, 'That I*
> *will send a famine on the land. Not a famine of bread, nor a*
> *thirst for water, but of hearing the words of the Lord.'"*
> Amos 8:11

> *"For the time will come when people will not tolerate sound doctrine*
> *and accurate instruction [that challenges them with God's truth]; but*
> *wanting to have their ears tickled [with something pleasing], they will*
> *accumulate for themselves [many] teachers [one after another, chosen]*
> *to satisfy their own desires and to support the errors they hold, and*
> *will turn their ears away from the truth and will wander off into*
> *myths and man-made fictions [and will accept the unacceptable].*
> *But as for you, be clear-headed in every situation [stay calm and*
> *cool and steady], endure every hardship [without flinching], do*
> *the work of an evangelist, fulfill [the duties of] your ministry."*
> 2 Timothy 4:3-5

After the Covid-19 pandemic, many pastors had to close their doors, and today we continue to see more people walking away from the Church. Many are being drawn to an easier path, a softer way of worship that feels convenient rather than being an active part of the body of Christ. But don't be alarmed. Jesus is still at work, pouring out His glory on His Church. When He comes for His bride, she will be pure, spotless, and without blemish.

I pray that you continue faithfully in the ministry God has called you to.

Search the scriptures, reading, studying, and meditating on it day and night. Offer yourself as an instrument for His service. Be alert, do not fall asleep.

Pray in faith, trusting the Holy Spirit, and listening to the voice of Christ who lives in you—the One who has sealed you until the day of His return.

DAY

9

PUT ON YOUR GARMENTS

"Yet regard the prayer of Your servant and his supplication,
O Lord my God, and listen to the cry and the prayer
which Your servant is praying before You today."
1 Kings 8:28

As long as the breath of God is in me and His Spirit rests upon my nostrils, my lips will not speak wickedness, nor will my tongue utter deceit. I will hold fast to righteousness and never let it go; my heart will not condemn me for as long as I live. I have clothed myself in righteousness; justice has been my robe and turban. May Your priests be clothed in righteousness, and your saints lift their voices in shouts of joy.

You said in Your Word

"Do not think that I have come to bring peace to the earth.
I have not come to bring peace, but a sword."
Matthew 10:34

"For the word of God is living and powerful, and sharper than any two-
edged sword, piercing even to the division of soul and spirit, and of joints
and marrow, and is a discerner of the thoughts and intents of the heart."
Hebrews 4:12

"So our hope is in the Lord. He is our help, our shield to protect us.
We rejoice in him, because we trust his holy name.
Lord, show your love to us as we put our hope in you."
Psalms 33:20-22

"Stay dressed for action and keep your lamps burning, and be like men
who are waiting for their master to come home from the wedding feast, so
that they may open the door to him at once when he comes and knocks.

Blessed are those servants whom the master finds awake when he comes. Truly, I say to you, he will dress himself for service and have them recline at table, and he will come and serve them. If he comes in the second watch, or in the third, and finds them awake, blessed are those servants! But know this, that if the master of the house had known at what hour the thief was coming, he[c] would not have left his house to be broken into. You also must be ready, for the Son of Man is coming at an hour you do not expect."
Luke 12:35-40

Let us be found ready when Christ appears.

DAY 10

SAME ACCESS

All believers share the same access to God, the same "code," through our faith in Jesus. Yet, there are some who need to encounter God's healing first, and through that touch of His love, their hearts are opened to truly hear the gospel and receive salvation.

"Jesus said to him, 'You people must see signs and
miracles before you will believe in me.'"
John 4:48

When Jesus hand-picked the twelve disciples, He sent them out with authority. Scripture tells us that they preached the message of the Kingdom of Heaven, healed the sick, cleansed lepers, raised the dead, and cast out demons.

"God saved us and called us to be holy, not because of what
we had done, but because of his own plan and kindness.
Before the world began, God planned that Christ Jesus
would show us God's kindness."
2 Timothy 1:9

God has called you.

"There are different kinds of working,
but in all of them and in everyone it is the same God at work."
1 Corinthians 12:6

Is it our own responsibility to find out what our gift and calling is?

"For just as each of us has one body with many members,
and these members do not all have the same function, so in Christ we,
though many, form one body, and each member belongs to all the others.

Our calling can bloom from other members in the body of Christ. Through the church we can find out what we are equipped to do for service to Christ Jesus our Lord.

THE CONDITION OF YOUR HOUSE

"When an evil spirit comes out of a person, it travels through dry places,
looking for a place to rest, but it doesn't find it. So the spirit says,
'I will go back to the house I left.' When the spirit comes back,
it finds the house still empty, swept clean, and made neat.
Then the evil spirit goes out and brings seven other spirits
even more evil than it is, and they go in and live there.
So the person has even more trouble than before.
It is the same way with the evil people who live today."
Matthew 12:43-45

An empty house shows a life without God's presence and His Word. Without Him, a person hasn't learned how to stand strong in spiritual battles, making them more open to the enemy's attacks.

When we stop growing in our faith, our spiritual lives begin to regress. Without fellowship with other believers and the support of the Church, we struggle to overcome the enemy. And when the Holy Spirit is not living within us, we are left to our own power and strength, making us an easy target for the devil's schemes.

"My friends, if someone is caught in any kind of wrongdoing,
those of you who are spiritual should set him right;
but you must do it in a gentle way. And keep an eye on yourselves,
so that you will not be tempted, too.
Help carry one another's burdens, and in this way
you will obey the law of Christ."
Galatians 6:1-2

*"To the weak I became weak, to win the weak.
I have become all things to all people so that by all
possible means I might save some."*
1 Corinthians 9:22

*"Therefore, put to death whatever is worldly in you: your sexual sin,
perversion, passion, lust, and greed (which is the
same thing as worshiping wealth).
It is because of these sins that God's anger comes on those who
refuse to obey him. You used to live that kind of sinful life.
Also get rid of your anger, hot tempers, hatred, cursing,
obscene language, and all similar sins. Don't lie to each other.
You've gotten rid of the person you used to be and the life you used to live,
and you've become a new person. This new person is continually
renewed in knowledge to be like its Creator."*
Colossians 3:5-10

Lord Jesus, help us put aside everything that is not from You. Teach us to stand together against Satan and his schemes, fighting in Your name, and clothed in the full armor of God. Empower us to be victorious, wise as serpents, and gentle as doves. Grant us discerning spirits so we may come to the aid of others and keep the evil one under our feet. Amen

12

SPEAK OUT

"Let the redeemed of the Lord say so,
whom He has redeemed from the hand of the adversary."
Psalms 107:2

Has the Lord redeemed you? Speak out!

Lord, You sealed my head on the day of battle. You keep me safe from the wicked. You are my strong deliverer. Your angels camp around me, protecting me from the wiles of the devil. You guard my entrance and my rear, giving me favor and light in every situation.

Lord, You have broken the bow and shattered the spear. Therefore, we do not fear; we trust in God, not in chariots. Our God is a consuming fire who destroys anything that tries to harm His children. He covers us under His wings, for He is our shelter, our King of kings, and Lord of lords. If God is for us, who can be against us? There is no other God.

He is the Alpha, He is the Omega, the beginning and the end. We bow down to the name of Jesus. Better is one day in His courts than a thousand elsewhere. Our God is awesome, our God reigns, and we reign with Him. We are seated with Him in heavenly places, and the weapons of our warfare are not carnal but mighty for pulling down strongholds, casting down every imagination that exalts itself against the knowledge of Christ, and bringing every thought into the obedience of Christ.

We are more than conquerors through Christ Jesus, who strengthens us. Greater is He who is in me than he who is in the world. For God's Spirit has joined with my spirit, affirming that I am a child of God. God saved me by His grace when I believed by faith. I have been made right in God's sight and have peace with God and my Lord Jesus Christ.

13

COMPLACENCY KILLS

We can't afford to just sit back and do nothing; complacency can't be our mindset. We can't let the distractions of this world get in the way of our relationship with God. That's why we need to pray without ceasing.

Our prayer life is powerful, it's like dynamite, and the Holy Spirit is the wick. The Word of God is the fire that lights it, guiding, teaching, correcting, transforming, and empowering us.

"Listen! I will come as a thief comes!
Blessed are those who stay awake and keep their clothes on
so that they will not walk around naked and have people see their shame."
Revelation 16:15

"I will search with lanterns in Jerusalem's darkest corners
to punish those who sit complacent in their sins.
They think the Lord will do nothing to them, either good or bad."
Zephaniah 1:12

"A crown to replace their ashes, and the oil of gladness to replace
their sorrow, and clothes of praise to replace their spirit of sadness. "
Isaiah 61:3a

"But you are a chosen race, a royal priesthood, a holy nation,
a people for his own possession, that you may proclaim the excellencies
of him who called you out of darkness into his marvelous light."
1 Peter 2:9

"What shall I return to the Lord for all his goodness to me?
I will lift up the cup of salvation and call on the name of the Lord.
I will fulfill my vows to the Lord in the presence of all his people."
Psalm 116:12-14

DAY
14

MORE ABUNDANTLY

When you speak God's Word and live by what He says, you will receive far more than you could ever ask or imagine, according to the power at work within you. That same resurrection power that raised Jesus from the dead is at work in you, just as Jesus declared.

> *"Truly, truly, I say to you, whoever believes in me will also*
> *do the works that I do; and greater works than these will he do,*
> *because I am going to the Father."*
> John 14:12

When you speak with the authority of Jesus' name, everything has to bow, every sickness, every disease, every demon must go.

> *"God sent the Son into the world not to condemn the world,*
> *but that the world through him might be saved."*
> John 3:17

Jesus saved you so you can share the good news with others and stand against the works of the devil. This is why the Son of God came: to destroy the works of the devil.

Christ has set us free, so let's live like it! Be who He's called you to be!

Do what Apostle Peter said:

> *"Live as people who are free, not using your freedom*
> *as a cover-up for evil, but living as servants of God."*
> 1 Peter 2:16

SPIRIT AND LETTER

"For in Christ Jesus you are all sons of God, through faith."
Galatians 3:26

"For God saved us and called us to live a holy life.
He did this, not because we deserved it, but because that was his plan
from before the beginning of time — to show
us his grace through Christ Jesus."
2 Timothy 1:9

Christ gave us His holiness—the more we live it, the more we become like Him!

The revealed Word of God is more than just what's written—it's living out what the Holy Spirit tells us to do. For example:

"The Lord said, 'Go out and stand on the mountain in the
presence of the Lord, for the Lord is about to pass by.'
Then a great and powerful wind tore the mountains apart
and shattered the rocks before the Lord, but the Lord was not in the wind.
After the wind there was an earthquake, but
the Lord was not in the earthquake.
After the earthquake came a fire, but the Lord was not in the fire.
And after the fire came a gentle whisper.
When Elijah heard it, he pulled his cloak over his face
and went out and stood at the mouth of the cave.
Then a voice said to him, 'What are you doing here, Elijah?'"
1 Kings 19:11-13

In Jesus name, we ask for more discernment to hear Your still small voice so we are where You want us. Help us exercise the authority that lives in us. We pray for wisdom by faith to make ourselves available to be used by You. Give us courage to fight for Your Kingdom until Your great and glorious return.

DAY
16

ENCOURAGEMENT

God is speaking encouragement into your spirit. He's building you up so you can step out and prophesy. Prayers and visions will come in unexpected moments. If you have ears to hear, wait on the Lord. He will show up with miracles, signs, and wonders.

The Lord Himself has made this promise, and nothing can break it.

"The Lord Almighty has sworn by his own life that he will bring many men to attack like a swarm of locusts, and they will shout with victory."
Jeremiah 51:14

Don't be afraid of the attacks that come against you, God has already raised a standard for you. The sword and the Word will come, bringing judgment through the grace God has given.

"Christ went and proclaimed to the spirits in prison, because they formerly did not obey, when God's patience waited in the days of Noah, while the ark was being prepared, in which a few, that is, eight persons, were brought safely through water. Baptism, which corresponds to this, now saves you, not as a removal of dirt from the body but as an appeal to God for a good conscience, through the resurrection of Jesus Christ."
1 Peter 3:19–21

"But you are a chosen race, a royal priesthood, a holy nation, a people for his own possession, that you may proclaim the excellencies of him who called you out of darkness into his marvelous light."
1 Peter 2:9

"For the message of the cross is foolishness to those who are perishing, but to us who are being saved it is the power of God.
1 Corinthians 1:18

"Brothers and sisters, think of what you were when you were called.
Not many of you were wise by human standards;
not many were influential;
not many were of noble birth. But God chose the foolish things of the
world to shame the wise; God chose the weak things of the world
to shame the strong. God chose the lowly things of this world and the
despised things—and the things that are not—to nullify the things that
are, so that no one may boast before him. It is because of him that you
are in Christ Jesus, who has become for us wisdom from God—that is,
our righteousness, holiness and redemption.
Therefore, as it is written: 'Let the one who boasts boast in the Lord.'"
1 Corinthians 1:26-31

DAY 17

SPIRIT OF FLATTERY

*"Woe to you when everyone speaks well of you,
for that is how their ancestors treated the false prophets."*
Luke 6:26

Today we can see the spirit of flattery at work. Many false teachers and voices avoid preaching repentance, and discipleship has been pushed to the side. The father of lies disguises himself as light, deceiving many with his lies.

"This is what the LORD Almighty says: 'Do not listen to what the prophets are prophesying to you; they fill you with false hopes. They speak visions from their own minds, not from the mouth of the LORD.'"
Jeremiah 23:16

The Gospel has been pushed to the background while the media has become the main source of answers. People are looking more to what man says than to what God's Word says. But all through the Bible, we see the warning against this and the instructions to follow God above all.

"Teach and urge these things."
1 Timothy 6:2

- Command and teach with confidence.
- Be an example to other believers, in your words, actions, love, faith, and purity.
- Stay devoted to reading Scripture publicly, encouraging others, and teaching.
- Don't neglect the gift God has given you.

If we have any platform or agenda other than God's Word in which we must obey, then we are doing what this scripture says:

> *"If anyone teaches otherwise and does not agree to the*
> *sound instruction of our Lord Jesus Christ and to godly teaching,*
> *they are conceited and understand nothing. They have an*
> *unhealthy interest in controversies and quarrels about*
> *words that result in envy, strife, malicious talk, evil suspicions*
> *and constant friction between people of corrupt mind,*
> *who have been robbed of the truth and who think*
> *that godliness is a means to financial gain."*
> 1 Timothy 6:3-5

NOT BY BREAD ALONE

We are saved by grace through faith in Jesus Christ. We're called to live
not by bread alone, but by every word that comes from God. In Him we
live, move, and have our being.

*"May the grace of the Lord Jesus Christ, and the love of God,
and the fellowship of the Holy Spirit be with you all."*
2 Corinthians 13:14

*"Instead, speaking the truth in love, we will grow to become
in every respect the mature body of him who is the head, that is, Christ."*
Ephesians 4:15

*"If I had cherished sin in my heart the Lord would have not listened,
but God has surely listened and has heard my prayer.
Praise to God who has not rejected my prayer
or withheld his love from me!"*
Psalm 66:18 -20

*"For everything God created is good and nothing is to be
rejected if it is received with thanksgiving because
it is consecrated by the word of God and prayer."*
1 Timothy 4:4-5

19

TRUST AND BE NOT AFRAID

*"Beloved, never avenge yourselves, but leave it to the wrath of God,
for it is written, 'Vengeance is mine, I will repay, says the Lord.'"*
Romans 12:19

O enemy, your destruction is finished forever! The face of the Lord is against those who do evil, cutting off their memory from the earth. Even if they go into captivity, God commands the sword against them. His eyes are set on their harm, not their good. But the Lord is with me like a mighty and awesome warrior. My persecutors will stumble; they will not prevail. They will be put to shame, and their lasting confusion will never be forgotten.

Lord of Hosts, You test the righteous and see the heart and mind. Let me see Your justice, for I have brought my case before You. And Lord, You promised in Your Word that You will keep me in perfect peace when my mind stays on You.

*"LORD, you establish peace for us; all that we
have accomplished you have done for us."*
Isaiah 26:12

God, my salvation, I will trust You and not be afraid. You, Lord, are my strength and my song; You have become my salvation. You are my God, and I will praise You; my father's God, and I will exalt You.

The Lord is a warrior; Holy is His name. Who is the King of Glory? The Lord, strong and mighty in battle! His name alone is God, the Most High over all the earth.

DAY

20

ENDURING HARDSHIP

*"The Lord was with Joseph, and he was a successful man; and he was in
the house of his master the Egyptian. And his master saw that the Lord
was with him and that the Lord made all he did to prosper in his hand.
So Joseph found favor in his sight and served him. Then he made him
overseer of his house, and all that he had he put under his authority."*
Genesis 39:2-4

Joseph was sold into slavery by his brothers and taken to Egypt. His
story is inspiring; it shows God's faithfulness through every high and
low. Joseph's life is a picture of steadiness and commitment. He truly
lived out what the Scriptures teach.

"If you want to be great in God's kingdom, learn to be the servant of all."
Matthew 20:26

Lord, You've called me to preach Your Word in every season. To
correct, rebuke, and encourage with patience, following Your divine
instructions. For Your Word says:

*"The time will come when people will not listen to the true teaching.
But people will find more and more teachers who please them.
They will find teachers who say what they want to hear."*
2 Timothy 4:3

Lord, You've told us to stay clear-minded in all things, to endure
hardship, to do the work of an evangelist, and to carry out our ministry.
You've called us to fight the good fight of faith and to take hold of
eternal life, the very charge You gave us.

Jesus, help us to obey God's commands and carefully follow His ways. Give us understanding and wisdom, so we may be wise as serpents and gentle as doves, spreading the gospel to all nations.

"If you want to test my teachings and discover where I received them, first be passionate to do God's will, and then you will be able to discern if my teachings are from the heart of God or from my own opinions."
John 7:17

GOD'S WORD NEVER CHANGES

"Jesus Christ is the same yesterday, today, and forever."
Hebrews 13:8

*"'Is not my word like fire?' declares the Lord, 'and like a hammer
which shatters a rock? Therefore behold, I am against the prophets,'
declares the Lord, 'who steal my words from each other.'"*
Jeremiah 23:29-30

*"'Both prophet and priest are godless; even in my temple I find their
wickedness,' declares the Lord. 'Therefore their path will become slippery;
they will be banished to darkness and there they will fall. I will bring
disaster on them in the year they are punished,' declares the Lord."*
Jeremiah 23:11-12

*"Do not think that I have come to bring peace on earth.
I have not come to bring peace, but a sword."*
Matthew 10:34

Jesus warned us to stay alert in these times, and the events unfolding now reflect what He said about peace.

Before Christ's birth, many Israelites expected that the coming of the Messiah would instantly bring peace and prosperity to their nation. Even Jesus' disciples may have held this belief. Through His teachings and miracles, Jesus revealed that He truly is the Messiah. However, He also wanted His followers to understand that an era of political peace was not about to begin.

Instead, His coming would stir division across the world. He said He came not to bring peace, but a sword. This "sword" does not represent God's judgment, military conflict, or personal violence. The Greek word used here—*machairan*—most often referred to large knives, such as those used by fishermen. These knives were meant for separating the parts of a catch or a cut of meat. In the same way, Scripture (as described in Hebrews) acts like that blade, dividing truth from error.

"The word of God is alive and active, sharper than any
double-edged sword. It cuts all the way through, to where soul
and spirit meet, to where joints and marrow come together.
It judges the desires and thoughts of the heart."
Hebrews 4:12

We are living in the very times Scripture warns about—when many will "fall away," be "led astray," "drawn away," "depart from the faith," and "follow destructive ways." Each of these phrases points to the same reality: turning against God and rejecting His truth.

"There were indeed false prophets among the people, just as there will be
false teachers among you. They will bring in destructive heresies,
even denying the Master who bought them, and will bring swift
destruction on themselves. Many will follow their depraved ways,
and the way of truth will be maligned because of them.
They will exploit you in their greed with made-up stories.
Their condemnation, pronounced long ago, is not idle,
and their destruction does not sleep.
For if God didn't spare the angels who sinned but cast them into hell,
and delivered them in chains of utter darkness to be kept for judgment."
2 Peter 2:1-4

"Because you're being so stubborn, and you're not sorry in your
heart for your sins, you're making God more and more angry with you.
The day of God's anger is coming.
Then he will pass judgment openly and fairly."
Romans 2:5

OUR LIVES PREACH

*"My message and my preaching were not with wise and
persuasive words, but with a demonstration of the Spirit's power."*
1 Corinthians 2:4

How we live is exactly what Paul was talking about in this scripture. Our lives preach a message whether we realize it or not, and God works in and through us.

The message He gives you is meant to reach someone that only you can reach. Everything you've gone through prepares you for your ministry. God uses it all, and He has chosen you to be the only glimpse of Jesus some people may ever see.

*"The Lord says, 'I will teach you the way you should go;
I will instruct you and advise you.'"*
Psalm 32:8

*"But as Scripture says: 'No eye has seen, no ear has heard,
and no mind has imagined the things that God has prepared
for those who love him.'"*
1 Corinthians 2:9

"Who put wisdom in the heart or gave understanding to the mind?"
Job 38:36

*"But there is a spirit within people,
the breath of the Almighty within them,
that makes them intelligent."*
Job 32:8

"Finally, be strong in the Lord and in his mighty power.
Put on the full armor of God, so that you can take your stand against
the devil's schemes. For our struggle is not against flesh and blood,
but against the rulers, against the authorities, against the powers of this
dark world and against the spiritual forces of evil in the heavenly realms.
Therefore put on the full armor of God, so that when the day of evil comes,
you may be able to stand your ground, and after
you have done everything, to stand.
Stand firm then, with the belt of truth buckled
around your waist, with the breastplate
of righteousness in place, and with your feet
fitted with the readiness that comes
from the gospel of peace. In addition to all this, take up the shield of faith,
with which you can extinguish all the flaming arrows of the evil one.
Take the helmet of salvation and the sword of
the Spirit, which is the word of God.
And pray in the Spirit on all occasions with
all kinds of prayers and requests.
With this in mind, be alert and always keep on
praying for all the Lord's people."
Ephesians 6:10-18

23

CREATING GIANTS

*"When the Lord saw how wicked everyone on earth was and
how evil their thoughts were all the time, he was sorry that he had ever
made them and put them on the earth. He was so filled with regret."*
Genesis 6:5-6

In today's world, people often create "giants" in their lives through disobedience, unbelief, and the lies of the enemy. In the days of Noah, evil spread across the earth when people turned away from God. But just as corruption grew then, God also provided a way of hope. What He desires for us now is to plant His Word deep in our hearts—so that we become "pregnant" with His Spirit, carrying His life within us.

Noah found grace in the eyes of the Lord, and through Jesus Christ, we have received that same grace. Yet, our conduct still matters. The way we live shapes our growth and shows who we truly are in Christ.

OUR CONDUCT AFFECTS GOD.

*"Do you think this passage means nothing?
It says, 'The Spirit that lives in us wants us to be his own.'"*
James 4:5

OUR CONDUCT IS VERY IMPORTANT TO GOD.

*"In the same way, there is more joy in heaven over one lost sinner
who repents and returns to God than over ninety-nine others
who are righteous and haven't strayed away!"*
Luke 15:7

OUR CONDUCT AFFECTS OTHERS.

"Do to others as you would like them to do to you."
Luke 6:31

OUR CONDUCT CAN INVITE SATAN IN OUR LIVES.

24

WALKING IN OBEDIENCE

The Word of Truth comes alive through faith as we walk in obedience to what God's Word tells us to do. We often pray for patience, but what we're truly asking for is endurance and perseverance; the strength to keep trusting God through every trial.

In the end, how we choose to respond to life's situations matters. Whether we respond in faith or in the flesh, each choice plants a seed, and every seed will produce a harvest in our lives.

"So don't lose your confidence in God, it will be richly rewarded. You need to be patient so that having done what God wants, you'll receive what he has promised. 'In just a little while he will come, as he said—he won't delay. Those who do what is right will live by trusting in God, and if they draw back from their commitment, I won't be pleased with them.' But we're not the kind of people who draw back and end up being lost. We are those who trust in God to save us."
Hebrews 10:35-39

"…knowing that the testing of your faith produces patience."
James 1:3

"Brothers, be patient until the Lord comes again. See how farmers wait for their precious crops to grow. They wait patiently for fall and spring rains. You, too, must be patient. Don't give up hope. The Lord will soon be here. Brothers, stop complaining about each other, or you will be condemned. Realize that the judge is standing at the door. Brothers, follow the example of the prophets who spoke in the name of the Lord. They were patient when they suffered unjustly. We consider those who endure to be blessed. You have heard about Job's endurance. You saw that the Lord ended Job's suffering because the Lord is compassionate and merciful. Above all things, my brothers, do not take an oath on anything in heaven or on earth. Do not take any oath. If you mean yes, say yes.

If you mean no, say no. Do this so that you won't be condemned. If any of you are having trouble, pray. If you are happy, sing psalms. If you are sick, call for the church leaders. Have them pray for you and anoint you with olive oil in the name of the Lord. (Prayers offered in faith will save those who are sick, and the Lord will cure them.) If you have sinned, you will be forgiven. So admit your sins to each other, and pray for each other so that you will be healed. Prayers offered by those who have God's approval are effective. Elijah was human like us. Yet, when he prayed that it wouldn't rain, no rain fell on the ground for three-and-a-half years. Then he prayed again. It rained, and the ground produced crops."
James 5:7-18

DAY

25

DEEPER TRUST AND OBEDIENCE

God often asks more of us. Just as He asked Abraham to sacrifice his son, God may call us to deeper trust and obedience, even when it feels costly. In Genesis 22, as Abraham prepared to sacrifice Isaac, the angel of the Lord stepped in and stopped him. God then provided a ram to take Isaac's place as the burnt offering.

"Now you, brothers and sisters, like Isaac, are children of promise."
Galatians 4:28

"The promises were spoken to Abraham and to his seed."
Galatians 3:16

Scripture does not say "and to seeds," meaning many people, but "and to your seed," meaning one person, who is Christ.

"Do you not know that your body is a temple of the Holy Spirit who is in you, whom you have received from God? You are not your own; you were bought at a price. Therefore glorify God with your body. We must stand firmly on God's Word and wait on Him, placing our hope completely in Him. When it seems like we hear nothing, it doesn't mean God is silent or still. Even in the quiet, He is at work, moving things into place so we can receive something greater than we imagined. His Word calls us to pause, to meditate, and to take in the Bread of Life, feeding our spirits with His promises. As we do, we gain wisdom and grace in our time of need. Our part is simple but powerful: to pray and to obey."
1 Corinthians 6:19-20

"For God alone, O my soul, wait in silence, for my hope is from him."
Psalms 62:5

"The Lord will fight for you; you need only to be still."
Exodus 14:14

"I wait for the Lord, my soul waits, and in his word I hope."
Psalm 130:5

"I wait for the Lord, my soul waits, and in his word I hope;
my soul waits for the Lord more than watchmen for the morning."
Psalm 130:5-6

"Therefore the Lord waits to be gracious to you, and therefore
he exalts himself to show mercy to you. For the Lord is a God
of justice; blessed are all those who wait for him."
Isaiah 30:18

DAY
26

LETTING GO

What you have or don't have does not define your destiny. Many times, we will not let go of what we do have so God can bless us with what He has for us. When we combine God's Word with obedience, He supplies all our needs. When we approach Him with an "all or nothing" attitude, fully surrendered and trusting, we make room for God to move powerfully and show Himself faithful in our lives.

See faith in action as Elijah obeys God:

"After a while the stream dried up because there was no rain. Then the Lord spoke his word to Elijah, 'Go to Zarephath in Sidon and live there. I have commanded a widow there to take care of you.' So Elijah went to Zarephath. When he reached the town gate, he saw a widow gathering wood for a fire. Elijah asked her, 'Would you bring me a little water in a cup so I may have a drink?' As she was going to get his water, Elijah said, 'Please bring me a piece of bread, too.' The woman answered, 'As surely as the Lord your God lives, I have no bread. I have only a handful of flour in a jar and only a little olive oil in a jug. I came here to gather some wood so I could go home and cook our last meal. My son and I will eat it and then die from hunger.' 'Don't worry,' Elijah said to her. 'Go home and cook your food as you have said. But first make a small loaf of bread from the flour you have, and bring it to me. Then cook something for yourself and your son. The Lord, the God of Israel, says, "That jar of flour will never be empty, and the jug will always have oil in it, until the day the Lord sends rain to the land."' So the woman went home and did what Elijah told her to do. And the woman and her son and Elijah had enough food every day. The jar of flour and the jug of oil were never empty, just as the Lord, through Elijah, had promised."
1 Kings 17:7-16

As we look at the widow's response in the story above, we can hear the deep cry of her heart. In her desperation, she confessed her faith declaring that only God could save her, and then she acted on what she believed.

Jesus, help us to be completely honest with You, just as the widow was. Teach us to receive Your Word with open hearts and a willing spirit, ready to give even our last for You. Open our spiritual eyes to see the endless supply of oil You provide through the Holy Spirit, renewing us and making each day fresh and full of Your presence. In Jesus name, amen.

DAY

27

PRAISE AND THANKSGIVING

Oh Lord, I bring to You an offering, the first fruits of my lips in praise and thanksgiving. I bow before You in humility and adoration, laying my heart at Your feet.

"Plead my cause and redeem me;
revive me according to Your word."
Psalm 119:154

"Turn away my eyes from looking at worthless things,
and revive me in Your way."
Psalms 119:37

"Revive me according to Your lovingkindness,
so that I may keep the testimony of Your mouth."
Psalms 119:88

"Will you not revive us again,
that your people may rejoice in you?"
Psalms 85:6

"For this is what the high and exalted One says— he who lives
forever, whose name is holy: "I live in a high and holy place, but
also with the one who is contrite and lowly in spirit, to revive the
spirit of the lowly and to revive the heart of the contrite."
Isaiah 57:15

My soul clings to the dust, revive me, O Lord, for Your name's sake. In Your righteousness, bring my soul out of trouble and breathe new life into me. Let Your mercy lift me from the weight of this world, that I may walk in Your strength and reflect Your glory.

HONORING GOD

The gift of honoring God often brings trials and challenges into our lives. Consider King David. Though he was chosen by God to be king, he first had to serve under a ruler chosen by the people, a man who sought to destroy him.

Before David reigned, he had to serve. He was called to honor someone who misused power for personal gain, a man who did not honor God or lead Israel with integrity. Yet, David remained faithful. He knew who he was in God, and he endured with humility and grace.

In the same way, we are called to be examples to the world around us. By showing patience, love, and honor, even when it's difficult, we reflect Christ to those who are lost. Through our obedience and character, others can be drawn to Him.

"So from now on we regard no one from a worldly point of view. Though we once regarded Christ in this way, we do so no longer. Therefore, if anyone is in Christ, the new creation has come: The old has gone, the new is here! All this is from God, who reconciled us to himself through Christ and gave us the ministry of reconciliation: that God was reconciling the world to himself in Christ, not counting people's sins against them. And he has committed to us the message of reconciliation. are therefore Christ's ambassadors, as though God were making his appeal through us. We implore you on Christ's behalf: Be reconciled to God. God made him who had no sin to be sin for us, so that in him we might become the righteousness of God."
2 Corinthians 5:16-21

WE ARE NOT ORDINARY PEOPLE

I am not an ordinary man. I am created by God, set apart for His purpose. Though I may face trials that feel unique, even in what feels ordinary or overwhelming, God is faithful. He provides the strength to endure and the way to overcome.

"No temptation has overtaken you except what is common to mankind. And God is faithful; he will not let you be tempted beyond what you can bear. But when you are tempted, he will also provide a way out so that you can endure it."
1 Corinthians 10:13

Endure what?

"For it has been granted to you on behalf of Christ not only to believe in him, but also to suffer for him."
Philippians 1:29

While we live on this earth, we will face suffering, but not without purpose. It is often through hardship that we learn what it means to administer the gospel, to live it out. Jesus said we would have trouble in this world, yet He also promised His peace and victory. As we faithfully endure, we administer His hope and truth to those who are watching.

What am I to administer?

"Now to each one the manifestation of the Spirit is given for the common good."
1 Corinthians 12:7

How can we add to the common good of the body of Christ?

*"So it is with you. Since you are eager for gifts of the Spirit,
try to excel in those that build up the church."*
1 Corinthians 14:12

That's why I search for the lost as if my very life depends on it, because my heart cannot rest while souls remain far from God. I live with a holy urgency, knowing that I have died to myself and now live only in Christ.

TAKE POSSESSION

"Look, I have taught you the laws and rules the Lord my God commanded me. Now you can obey the laws in the land you are entering, in the land you will take. Obey these laws carefully, in order to show the other nations that you have wisdom and understanding. When they hear about these laws, they will say, 'This great nation of Israel is wise and understanding.' No other nation is as great as we are. Their gods do not come near them, but the Lord our God comes near when we pray to him. And no other nation has such good teachings and commands as those I am giving to you today. But be careful! Watch out and don't forget the things you have seen. Don't forget them as long as you live, but teach them to your children and grandchildren."
Deuteronomy 4:5-9

The Lord wants to speak to us out of the fire. The Holy Spirit burns within us, constantly guiding us in communion with God, hoping that we will listen to His Word and receive His instructions.

God is calling us to keep idols from entering our lives. Our bodies are temples of the Holy Spirit. We cannot ignore the power of God within us or excuse sinful behavior as "just the flesh," for we are born of the Spirit.

It's time to act like children of God, time to say yes to the Holy Spirit and no to evil desires. The fear of the Lord is true wisdom, and true understanding is to ignore evil.

DAY
31

HUNGER FOR GOD

"Therefore, as God's chosen people, holy and dearly loved,
clothe yourselves with compassion, kindness,
humility, gentleness and patience."
Colossians 3:12

God wants us to be humble and hungry.

"Finally, all of you, be like-minded, be sympathetic,
love one another, be compassionate and humble."
1 Peter 3:8

We must hunger for God, seeking times alone with Him just as Jesus did. Go into your "closet," away from distractions, and spend time in the presence of our Father in Heaven. In these quiet moments, our hearts are renewed, and we draw closer to Him.

"Blessed are those who hunger and thirst for righteousness,
for they will be filled."
Matthew 5:6

Father, fill us in Jesus' name and give us a deep desire to seek You wholeheartedly. Help us to worship You with all that we are, heart, soul, and spirit.

A NEW LIFE

"Touch not my anointed ones, do my prophets no harm!"
Psalm 105:15

David recognized that Saul, despite his position as king, was still under God's authority. Even when Saul turned against him and sought to kill him, David could see the enemy's schemes and he trusted God's plan above all.

God's Word tells us to no longer be ignorant to Satan's schemes.

"No longer, then, do we judge anyone by human standards.
Even if at one time we judged Christ according to human
standards, we no longer do so. Anyone who is joined to Christ
is a new being; the old is gone, the new has come."
2 Corinthians 5:16-17

We don't look at people from a human point of view anymore. There was a time when we even saw Christ that way, but now we understand who He truly is. Anyone who belongs to Christ becomes a new person and is given a fresh start and a new life. We also recognize that our battles aren't against other people, but against unseen spiritual forces, real powers of darkness and evil at work in this world.

We put on God's armor, and He fights our battles. When we obey Him, we are fighting the good fight of faith.

"For the weapons of our warfare are not merely human, but they
have divine power to destroy strongholds. We destroy arguments
and every proud obstacle raised up against the knowledge of
God, and we take every thought captive to obey Christ."
2 Corinthians 10:4-5

David lived by faith like this:

*"Look at the proud person. He is not right in himself.
But the righteous person will live because of his faithfulness."*
Habakkuk 2:4

DAY
33

LIVE BY FAITH

Being faithful to the leaders God has placed over us is one way we show that we live by faith. If we cannot honor and obey those God has anointed to lead, how can we truly obey God's commands?

"Saul sent David to fight in different battles, and David was very successful. Then Saul put David over the soldiers, which pleased Saul's officers and all the other people. After David had killed the Philistine, he and the men returned home. Women came out from all the towns of Israel to meet King Saul. They sang songs of joy, danced, and played tambourines and stringed instruments. As they played, they sang, 'Saul has killed thousands of his enemies, but David has killed tens of thousands.'"
1 Samuel 18:5-7

When we start wanting what God gave to someone else more than we want God Himself, our focus shifts. Instead of walking confidently in who we are in Christ and serving God with the gifts and abilities He has given us, we get distracted by comparison and envy. This doesn't just slow down our calling; it can destroy it. When we step out of God's will and try to operate outside the lane He created for us, we end up in disobedience. This is what scripture says happened:

"The women's song upset Saul, and he became very angry. He thought, 'The women say David has killed tens of thousands, but they say I have killed only thousands. The only thing left for him to have is the kingdom!' So Saul watched David closely from then on, because he was jealous."
1 Samuel 18:8-9

HAVING A RIGHT SPIRIT

Lord Jesus, keep the right spirit within us. Help us be like Jonathan, who made a covenant with David and loved him as he loved himself. Let our love, Lord, be a fire that pleases You, seeking not success, position, or recognition, but simply serving You with a pure and willing heart.

We offer our lives to You as a living sacrifice, holy and pleasing to You alone. This is our true and reasonable act of worship. May we honor You in obedience, humility, and love, staying in Your will and walking in the calling You have given us. Amen.

"Jonathan took off the robe he was wearing and gave it to David, along with his tunic, and even his sword, his bow and his belt."
1 Samuel 18:4

"Saul told his son Jonathan and all his officials that he planned to kill David. But Jonathan was very fond of David, and so he told him, 'My father is trying to kill you. Please be careful tomorrow morning; hide in some secret place and stay there.'"
1 Samuel 19:1-2

David continued to declare the following words every day as he waited for God to avenge him and protect him from Saul, who sought his life.

"The Lord is my light and my salvation, whom shall I fear? The Lord is the stronghold of my life, of whom shall I be afraid? When the wicked advance against me to devour me, it is my enemies and my foes who will stumble and fall. Though an army besiege me, my heart will not fear; though war break out against me, even then I will be confident. One thing I ask from the Lord, this only do I seek: that I may dwell in the house of the Lord all the days of my life, to gaze on the beauty of the Lord and to

seek him in his temple. For in the day of trouble he will keep me safe in his dwelling; he will hide me in the shelter of his sacred tent and set me high upon a rock. Then my head will be exalted above the enemies who surround me; at his sacred tent I will sacrifice with shouts of joy; I will sing and make music to the Lord. Hear my voice when I call, Lord; be merciful to me and answer me. My heart says of you, 'Seek his face!' Your face, Lord, I will seek. Do not hide your face from me, do not turn your servant away in anger; you have been my helper. Do not reject me or forsake me, God my Savior. Though my father and mother forsake me, the Lord will receive me. Teach me your way, Lord; lead me in a straight path because of my oppressors. Do not turn me over to the desire of my foes, for false witnesses rise up against me, spouting malicious accusations. I remain confident of this: I will see the goodness of the Lord in the land of the living. Wait for the Lord; be strong and take heart and wait for the Lord."
Psalms 27:1-14

DAY
35
PROPHET OF GOD

"Before the Lord God does anything,
he tells his plans to his servants the prophets."
Amos 3:7

"As Samuel grew up, the Lord was with him, and everything Samuel said
proved to be reliable. And all Israel, from Dan in the north to Beersheba
in the south, knew that Samuel was confirmed as a prophet of the Lord."
1 Samuel 3:19-20

So what did God call Samuel to do next? He called him to declare God's word to Israel. After Samuel's anointing came God's judgment. The Israelites had disobeyed God. They chose a king over God, and God gave them what they asked for. But He also warned them of what their future would look like as a result of their choice.

"So Samuel passed on the LORD's warning to the people who were asking
him for a king. 'This is how a king will reign over you,' Samuel said.
'The king will draft your sons and assign them to his chariots and his
charioteers, making them run before his chariots. Some will be generals
and captains in his army,[a] some will be forced to plow in his fields
and harvest his crops, and some will make his weapons and chariot
equipment. The king will take your daughters from you and force them
to cook and bake and make perfumes for him. He will take away the
best of your fields and vineyards and olive groves and give them to his
own officials. He will take a tenth of your grain and your grape harvest
and distribute it among his officers and attendants. He will take your
male and female slaves and demand the finest of your cattle and donkeys
for his own use. He will demand a tenth of your flocks, and you will
be his slaves. When that day comes, you will beg for relief from this
king you are demanding, but then the LORD will not help you.'"
1 Samuel 8:10-18

"For no one can ever be made right with God
by doing what the law commands.
The law simply shows us how sinful we are."
Romans 3:20

"For prophecy never had its origin in the human will,
but prophets, though human, spoke from God
as they were carried along by the Holy Spirit."
2 Peter 1:21

GOD KNOWS OUR HEART

*"And the Lord said to Samuel, 'Listen to the voice of the people
in all that they say to you; for they have not rejected you, but
they have rejected me from being king over them.'"*
1 Samuel 8:7

Even though Israel rejected Samuel, God gave them what they asked for.
God knew they were afraid; he knew their hearts.

*"The day before Saul came, the Lord had told Samuel: 'About this
time tomorrow I will send you a man from the land of Benjamin.
Appoint him to lead my people Israel. He will save my people from the
Philistines. I have seen the suffering of my people, and I have listened
to their cries.' When Samuel first saw Saul, the Lord said to Samuel,
'This is the man I told you about. He will organize my people.'"*
1 Samuel 9:15–17

Samuel obeyed God, even though He knew it was a mistake to make
Saul their king. He then gave the people this Word of encouragement
and rebuke.

*"Then Samuel said to the people, 'The Lord, who appointed Moses and
Aaron and who brought your ancestors up from the land of Egypt, is a
witness. Now present yourselves, so I may confront you before the Lord
about all the righteous acts he has done for you and your ancestors. 'When
Jacob went to Egypt, your ancestors cried out to the Lord, and he sent them
Moses and Aaron, who led your ancestors out of Egypt and settled them
in this place. But they forgot the Lord their God, so he handed them over
to Sisera, commander of the army of Hazor, to the Philistines, and to the
king of Moab. These enemies fought against them. Then they cried out
to the Lord and said, "We have sinned, for we abandoned the Lord and
worshiped the Baals and the Ashtoreths. Now rescue us from the power of*

1 Samuel 12:6–17

Our words matter—they can bring life or death. When we don't keep our word, it has consequences. But God's word is always true and powerful. You can trust it completely.

GOD IS FAITHFUL
TO HIS WORD

"David and all Israel were celebrating with all their might before the Lord, with castanets, harps, lyres, timbrels, sistrums and cymbals. When they came to the threshing floor of Nakon, Uzzah reached out and took hold of the ark of God, because the oxen stumbled. The Lord's anger burned against Uzzah because of his irreverent act; therefore God struck him down, and he died there beside the ark of God."
2 Samuel 6:5-7

As I reflected upon this story this scripture came to mind:

"It is a terrible thing to fall into the hands of the living God."
Hebrews 10:31

God will never go against His own Word. What He speaks will always come to pass, His Word will never return void without accomplishing what He said.

How many times have we found ourselves in error, yet God's grace still carried us? When I think about Uzzah reaching out to touch the Ark, I see a warning about treating the things of God casually. I realized I was doing the same thing, and like Uzzah, I learned a hard lesson about obedience. But I thank God for His mercy. He never stopped convicting me, never stopped speaking to me, until I finally repented and obeyed. Only then did I begin to experience His favor and peace again.

Uzzah's prophetic destiny was to carry the Ark of the Lord. In the same way, your destiny has been ordained by God. He is the One who called you, and He is the One who will give you the power to fulfill what He has spoken over your life. Your only responsibility is to remain faithful.

Continue to abide in Him. Walk in obedience to what the Holy Spirit has spoken to you. Do not get distracted by accomplishments, titles, or outward success. Do not compare your progress to someone else's calling. Stay focused on what God has assigned to you. Keep carrying your cross daily for the glory of God. Keep serving, keep trusting, keep obeying, even when no one sees. God will reveal what He has placed inside you, and He will use your life powerfully for His Kingdom.

DIVINE ORDER

God has a divine order, and only He knows the day of Christ's return and those who will ultimately be saved. God has already revealed the signs that will take place before the end. We can clearly see the evidence that His return is drawing closer. The Bible says, "In the latter times, some will depart from the faith."

God is pouring out His Spirit on His Church, and we are the generation that will experience a fresh and powerful anointing to reach the lost. The Holy Spirit is stirring hearts, awakening callings, and positioning His people with purpose.

"Now to him who is able to do immeasurably more than all
we ask or imagine, according to his power that is at work
within us, to him be glory in the church and in Christ Jesus
throughout all generations, for ever and ever! Amen."
Ephesians 3:20-21

"For we are to God the pleasing aroma of Christ among those
who are being saved and those who are perishing.
To the one we are an aroma
that brings death; to the other, an aroma that brings life.
And who is equal to such a task? Unlike so many, we do not
peddle the word of God for profit. On the contrary, in Christ
we speak before God with sincerity, as those sent from God."
2 Corinthians 2:15-17

The word of God says Christ will not return until all He has chosen for salvation come to faith.

"Truly I tell you, this generation will certainly not
pass away until all these things have happened."
Mark 13:30

What things?

*"And the Good News about the Kingdom will be preached
throughout the whole world, so that all nations will hear it;
and then the end will come."*
Matthew 24:14

DAY
39

OPERATING UNDER
HIS AUTHORITY

"Now the Lord is the Spirit, and where the Spirit of the Lord is, there is freedom. And we all, who with unveiled faces contemplate the Lord's glory, are being transformed into his image with ever-increasing glory, which comes from the Lord, who is the Spirit."
2 Corinthians 3:17–18

You cannot cast out demons unless you are truly sent by Jesus and operate under His authority, His anointing, and the power of the Holy Spirit. Deliverance is not a human ability; it is a spiritual work that comes from God alone. Without a real relationship with Jesus, you have no true authority in the spiritual realm.

"Many will say to me on that day, 'Lord, Lord, didn't we prophesy in your name? Didn't we force out demons and do many miracles by the power and authority of your name?' Then I will tell them publicly, 'I've never known you. Get away from me, you evil people.'"
Matthew 7:22-23

We must follow Christ, not just do whatever we want. Everything we do must come from a place of faith and a real relationship with Jesus.

"But people who aren't spiritual can't receive these truths from God's Spirit. It all sounds foolish to them and they can't understand it, for only those who are spiritual can understand what the Spirit means."
1 Corinthians 2:14

We must keep things in the right perspective, the gifts of casting out demons and performing miracles are not for entertainment. They exist for one purpose alone: to glorify God.

Years ago, I visited a Holiness church and witnessed people laying hands on others in ministry. I didn't fully understand the purpose or the spiritual responsibility behind it, but I began to imitate what I saw. The pastor eventually pulled me aside and told me to stop. At first, I didn't understand why, but now I do. Ministry must be led by the Holy Spirit, not by imitation or emotion.

What God desires most from us is repentance and obedience. If we continue to live in sin while trying to serve God publicly, we become a bad witness to others. Our actions end up saying more than our words.

DAY

40

PURE LOVE

After David received more praise that Saul, scripture says:

*"Saul became very angry because he considered this saying to be
insulting. 'To David they credit tens of thousands,' he said, 'but to
me they credit only a few thousand. The only thing left for David
is my kingdom.' From that day on Saul kept an eye on David."*
1 Samuel 18: 8-9

Lord Jesus, keep our hearts right before You. Help us walk with
the same loyalty and love as Jonathan, who made a covenant with David
and loved him as himself.

*"Jonathan took off the robe he was wearing and gave it to David,
along with his tunic, and even his sword, his bow and his belt."*
1 Samuel 18:4

Lord, ignite our hearts with a pure love for You, a love that seeks
Your will above everything else, not striving for status or self, but serving
You with complete devotion.

*"So brothers and sisters, since God has shown us great mercy, I beg you to
offer your lives as a living sacrifice to him. Your offering must be only for
God and pleasing to him, which is the spiritual way for you to worship."*
Romans 12:1

DAY

41

PROPHETIC WARS

"'I also raised up prophets from among your children and Nazirites from among your youths. Is this not true, people of Israel?' declares the Lord. 'But you made the Nazirites drink wine and commanded the prophets not to prophesy. Now then, I will crush you as a cart crushes when loaded with grain. The swift will not escape, the strong will not muster their strength, and the warrior will not save his life. The archer will not stand his ground, the fleet-footed soldier will not get away, and the horseman will not save his life. Even the bravest warriors will flee naked on that day,' declares the Lord."
Amos 2:11-16

Throughout Scripture, God has declared that these events will take place, and we can see the signs all around us, pointing to His return. Though in these latter days some will fall away from the faith, be encouraged; we have been chosen and equipped for such a time as this. Let us stand firm, encouraged by His promises and faithful to our calling.

"Now to him who is able to do immeasurably more than all we ask or imagine, according to his power that is at work within us, to him be glory in the church and in Christ Jesus throughout all generations, for ever and ever! Amen."
Ephesians 3:20-21

God is pouring out His Spirit upon the Church in many ways, and we are the generation chosen to walk in this anointing of the Holy Spirit to reach the lost. We are being awakened, empowered, and divinely positioned, placed in communities, workplaces, and nations to fulfill His purpose in this hour.

"For we are the aroma of Christ to God among those who are being saved and among those who are perishing, to one a fragrance from death to

death, to the other a fragrance from life to life. Who is sufficient for these things? For we are not, like so many, peddlers of God's word, but as men of sincerity, as commissioned by God, in the sight of God we speak in Christ."
2 Corinthians 2:15-17

Even now, deceiving spirits are all around, seeking to lure others into taking the easy path, one that changes the Word of God by adding to it or taking away from it. These spirits masquerade as light, whispering lies that invite compromise and sow seeds of unbelief. They aim to build strongholds in the spiritual realm and atmosphere, declaring that prophecy is dead and belonged only to generations past. Some even claim that the gifts of the Spirit are no longer accessible, suggesting they were reserved solely for the people of biblical times.

"'The days are coming,' declares the Sovereign Lord, 'when I will send a famine through the land— not a famine of food or a thirst for water, but a famine of hearing the words of the Lord.'"
Amos 8:11

"For the time will come when people will not tolerate sound doctrine and accurate instruction [that challenges them with God's truth]; but wanting to have their ears tickled [with something pleasing], they will accumulate for themselves [many] teachers [one after another, chosen] to satisfy their own desires and to support the errors they hold, and will turn their ears away from the truth and will wander off into myths and man-made fictions [and will accept the unacceptable]. But as for you, be clear-headed in every situation [stay calm and cool and steady], endure every hardship [without flinching], do the work of an evangelist, fulfill [the duties of] your ministry."
2 Timothy 4:3-5

As I prayed and meditated on these passages, I was stirred to reflect on the profound transition unfolding within the Church.

In the wake of the coronavirus pandemic, many pastors closed their doors, and even now, countless believers are drifting away, deceived into embracing a more comfortable, diluted form of worship. They choose convenience over commitment, preferring a personalized faith rather than being active members of the body of Christ.

But do not be alarmed. Christ is preparing to pour out His future glory upon His Church. He is coming for His Bride, spotless, without blemish, purified through fire and faith.

Continue to fulfill the ministries God has entrusted to you. Search the Scriptures, meditate on them day and night, and offer yourselves as living instruments for His service.

Do not fall asleep or be drawn away by temptation. Pray in faith, led by the Holy Spirit, and listen for the voice of Christ within you, The One in whom you have been sealed until the day of His return.

DAY

42

WASTED TIME

The giants of social media seek to consume our time, flooding our minds with fear, uncertainty, and endless distractions, all designed to pull our focus away from Christ. They stir panic in the hearts of the masses, manipulating imaginations until they murmur with worry, complain in confusion, and begin to question their faith. But God has spoken clearly:

"Therefore, since we have these promises, dear friends, let us purify ourselves from everything that contaminates body and spirit, perfecting holiness out of reverence for God."
2 Corinthians 7:1

"For if there was glory in that which lasted for a while, how much more glory is there in that which lasts forever! Because we have this hope, we are very bold."
2 Corinthians 3:11-12

"Keep a close watch on how you live and on your teaching. Stay true to what is right for the sake of your own salvation and the salvation of those who hear you."
1 Timothy 4:16

"Do this because we live in an important time. It is now time for you to wake up from your sleep, because our salvation is nearer now than when we first believed. The "night" is almost finished, and the "day" is almost here. So we should stop doing things that belong to darkness and take up the weapons used for fighting in the light."
Romans 13:11-12

"Do not be unequally yoked with unbelievers. For what do righteousness and lawlessness have in common? And what fellowship does light have

with darkness? And what union does Christ have with Belial? Or what part does a believer have with an unbeliever? And what agreement is there between a temple of God and idols? For you are a temple of the living God, exactly as God said: 'I will dwell in them and walk in them; and I will be their God, and they shall be My people. Therefore, come out from the midst of them and be separate,' says the Lord, 'and touch not the unclean, and I will receive you; [18] And I shall be a Father to you, and you shall be My sons and daughters,' says the Lord Almighty."
2 Corinthians 6:14-18

PRAYER OF DECLARATION

We declare in the mighty name of Jesus: we will not be swayed by the lies of the enemy. We refuse to participate in the deception spread through social media and news outlets that promote fear, confusion, and false narratives. These voices attempt to overshadow the power of the blood of Christ, and the true eternal Word of God. We stand firm. We fix our eyes on Jesus and boldly declare that His truth will prevail.

DAY

43

PROPHETIC DESTINIES

*"Now the springs of the deep and the floodgates of the heavens
had been closed, and the rain had stopped falling from the sky."*
Genesis 8:2

Prophetic destinies are awakening. Every moment, I am choosing My warriors. Sharpen your spirits. Equip your senses to see clearly in the heat of battle. I am training you for My future glory, taking what is Mine and declaring it to you. Come out from among the hecklers, the sayers, the watchers—those who wage warfare in your minds. They poison souls with witchcraft and sorcery, twisting truth into lies through debate and argument. Awaken to the sound of the spiritual trumpet, it has already sounded.

Take your post, mighty men of old. You were predestined to watch, to war, and to win. Take your post again, mighty men of old, for you are called to watch and to pray. Do not listen with earthly ears. Heaven is the city with foundations, whose builder and maker is God.

*"For Abraham was waiting for the city which God has
designed and built, the city with permanent foundations."*
Hebrews 11:10

*"Then I looked and heard the voice of many angels,
numbering thousands upon thousands, and
ten thousand times ten thousand.
They encircled the throne and the living creatures and the elders."*
Revelation 5:11

*"The angel of the Lord encamps all around those
who fear Him, and delivers them."*
Psalms 34:7

44

YOUR LIFE IS THE THUMBPRINT OF GOD

Read Luke 24:13-31.

> *"The chief priests and our rulers handed him over to be sentenced to death, and they crucified him; but we had hoped that he was the one who was going to redeem Israel. And what is more, it is the third day since all this took place."*
> Luke 24:20-21

Maybe you are like the two in this passage. You've met Jesus, you've experienced Jesus, but you too are still hoping for the third day. Not fully living in the resurrection power.

Perhaps your life has handicapped you to a permanent address you do not wish to reside. Maybe you have a mental or physical disability that keeps you from being who you would like to be. Maybe you are jobless, homeless, or are an ex-con who just needs a second chance. Maybe you are an outcast to the social norms of this society because of your outward appearance. Or how about an abused woman who has no way out and is hopeless. Or an alcoholic or junkie who can't kick the habit.

Whatever the situation, it's not too big for God. Your life is a thumbprint, formed by God, created to be His voice that calls to the world and says, "There is something different about this guy." Why? This is the unique gift that draws others to you: your individuality.

The call in your life may be to stay. Waiting on God is an act of obedience that exercises your faith. It prepares you and equips you with the power of the Holy Spirit

45

AWAKENING

When we hear God's Word, our spiritual eyes are opened and we receive revelation, heavenly truth that feeds our souls. This spiritual "meat" is the will of God for our lives. When we feed our spirit with the Word of God, we receive supernatural wisdom, strength, healing, and direction. God equips us not only for our own growth, but so we can also bless others with what He has given us.

Romans 10:17 says faith comes by hearing and hearing by the word of God.

"One day Peter and John were going up to the temple at the time of prayer—at three in the afternoon. Now a man who was lame from birth was being carried to the temple gate called Beautiful, where he was put every day to beg from those going into the temple courts. When he saw Peter and John about to enter, he asked them for money. Peter looked straight at him, as did John. Then Peter said, 'Look at us!' So the man gave them his attention, expecting to get something from them. Then Peter said, 'Silver or gold I do not have, but what I do have I give you. In the name of Jesus Christ of Nazareth, walk.' Taking him by the right hand, he helped him up, and instantly the man's feet and ankles became strong. He jumped to his feet and began to walk. Then he went with them into the temple courts, walking and jumping, and praising God."
Acts 3:1-8

When we speak the name of Jesus with faith, just like Peter did, miracles happen. But it doesn't stop there. When the person receiving the word also responds in faith, the power of God is released. That's exactly what we see in Acts 3: the man who had been lame from birth believed, received strength in his legs, and immediately began walking, jumping, and praising God. His miracle became a testimony that drew others to Christ.

This scripture reminds us to listen to what the Spirit is saying. If we want to be used by God, we must make ourselves available and active in the Body of Christ.

KEEPING A SOUND MIND

"Jesus answered, 'My teaching is not my own.
It comes from the one who sent me.
Anyone who chooses to do the will of God will find out
whether my teaching comes from God or whether I speak on my own.'"
John 7:16-17

"The Lord was with Joseph so that he prospered, and he lived in the house
of his Egyptian master. When his master saw that the Lord was with him
and that the Lord gave him success in everything he did, Joseph found
favor in his eyes and became his attendant. Potiphar put him in charge
of his household, and he entrusted to his care everything he owned."
Genesis 39:2-4

Joseph was sold into slavery by his own brothers and sent to Egypt. His story is one of incredible faith and perseverance, a powerful reminder of God's faithfulness through every trial. Though Joseph faced many ups and downs, his life displayed unwavering commitment and trust in God. He lived out the very principle Jesus taught:

"If you want to be great in God's kingdom, you must be the servant of all"
Matthew 20:26

You have entrusted me, O Lord, to preach Your Word in every season, to be ready at all times. You have called me to correct, to rebuke, and to encourage with patience and humility, walking in obedience to Your divine instruction.

"For the time will come when people will not put up with sound doctrine.
Instead, to suit their own desires, they will gather around them
a great number of teachers to say what their itching ears want to hear."
2 Timothy 4:3

Lord, You have told us to keep a sound mind and to stay steady in all things, to endure hardship, to do the work of an evangelist, and to faithfully carry out the ministry You've given us.

You have called us to fight the good fight of faith and to take hold of eternal life, just as we agreed when You gave us this holy charge.

Jesus, help us to obey the commands of God and to walk carefully in His ways. Give us understanding and divine wisdom so that we may be wise as serpents and gentle as doves, spreading the gospel of Your Kingdom to all nations. Amen.

CLOTHED IN RIGHTEOUSNESS

I put on righteousness, and it covered me; justice was my robe and my turban.

Lord, clothe Your priests with righteousness, and let Your saints lift their voices in joyful praise!

*"Yet give attention to your servant's prayer and his plea
for mercy, Lord my God. Hear the cry and the prayer that
your servant is praying in your presence this day."*
1 Kings 8:28

*"As long as I have life within me, the breath of God in my nostrils,
my lips will not say anything wicked, and my tongue will not utter
lies. I will never admit you are in the right; till I die, I will not
deny my integrity. I will maintain my innocence and never let go
of it; my conscience will not reproach me as long as I live."*
Job 27:3-6

"I did not come to bring peace, but a sword."
Matthew 10:34b

*"For the word of God is alive and active. Sharper than any
double-edged sword, it penetrates even to dividing soul and spirit,
joints and marrow; it judges the thoughts and attitudes of the heart."*
Hebrews 4:12

*"We put our hope in the Lord. He is our help and our shield. In
him our hearts rejoice, for we trust in his holy name. Let your
unfailing love surround us, Lord, for our hope is in you alone."*
Psalms 33:20-22

"Be dressed for service and keep your lamps burning, as though you were waiting for your master to return from the wedding feast. Then you will be ready to open the door and let him in the moment he arrives and knocks. The servants who are ready and waiting for his return will be rewarded. I tell you the truth, he himself will seat them, put on an apron, and serve them as they sit and eat! He may come in the middle of the night or just before dawn. But whenever he comes, he will reward the servants who are ready. 'Understand this: If a homeowner knew exactly when a burglar was coming, he would not permit his house to be broken into. You also must be ready all the time, for the Son of Man will come when least expected.'"
Luke 12:35-40

DAY

48

VICTORIOUS

O God, teach me to rule over my flesh, so that when unexpected events come, I can still recognize that You are at work. Help me to stand on Your Word and humbly admit when I am wrong, without blaming myself or others. Teach me to choose forgiveness over condemnation, allowing Your grace to do its perfect work in me. Even when it hurts, I know my love for You is stronger than any wrong choice or mistake I've made, for You cause all things to work together for the good of those who love You. Nothing, absolutely nothing, can separate me from Your love. Amen.

LIVING IN THE NEW

If we could truly grasp how blessed we are, our whole perspective would change. We must stop looking through a carnal lens and allow the Spirit of God to put to death the old way we see ourselves, the person we were in the past. We can't keep letting Satan drag us down with lies that bring condemnation, guilt, and shame.

Instead, we need to hear and believe what God's Word says, above every other voice, above every feeling, above every past mistake. His truth defines who we are now, not our failures.

"I the Lord do not change. So you, the descendants
of Jacob, are not destroyed."
Malachi 3:6

"God is not like people. He tells no lies. He is not like humans.
He doesn't change his mind. When he says something, he does
it. When he makes a promise, he keeps it. I have received a
command to bless. He has blessed, and I can't change it."
Numbers 23:19-20

What Christ has done for us on the cross by His blood and death and resurrection, the curse is dead and we are alive in Him.

"Praise be to the God and Father of our Lord Jesus Christ, who has
blessed us in the heavenly realms with every spiritual blessing in
Christ. For he chose us in him before the creation of the world to be
holy and blameless in his sight. In love he predestined us for adoption
to sonship through Jesus Christ, in accordance with his pleasure and
will to the praise of his glorious grace, which he has freely given us in
the One he loves. In him we have redemption through his blood, the
forgiveness of sins, in accordance with the riches of God's grace."
Ephesians 1:3-7

STOP BELIEVING THE LIES OF SATAN!

Peter believed the lies of Satan, that he could take the place of Jesus and die so that Jesus might live. But only Jesus could die for the sins of the world. Peter also believed that he would never deny Christ, yet before the rooster crowed, he denied Him three times, just as Jesus said.

In the same way, Satan often plants thoughts in our minds to distract us from the truth of God's Word and from what Jesus has already spoken. He tries to convince us that we can do things our own way or that our strength is enough. But Jesus calls us to something greater, to deny ourselves, take up our cross, and follow Him.

We must crucify our own desires and surrender our will to Christ's will, trusting that His plan is always better than ours.

"I do not understand what I do. For what I want to do I do not do, but what I hate I do. And if I do what I do not want to do, I agree that the law is good. As it is, it is no longer myself who do it, but it is sin living in me. For I know that good itself does not dwell in me, that is, in my sinful nature. For I have the desire to do what is good, but I cannot carry it out. For I do not do the good I want to do, but the evil I do not want to do—this I keep on doing. Now if I do what I do not want to do, it is no longer I who do it, but it is sin living in me that does it."
Romans 7:15-20

It is the Holy Spirit who works in us to do the will of God, and He is the One who carries it out through us. So stop letting Satan condemn you. Jesus has already paid for your sins in full. Walk in the newness of life that is found in Christ!

Bring your sins and struggles to the throne of grace and ask Jesus to take away the things you hate to keep doing. Look into the perfect law of liberty, the freedom Christ has given you and remember that you are no longer bound by the flesh.

You are born of the Spirit, not of the flesh. Therefore, walk in the Spirit, and you will not fulfill the desires of the flesh.

DAY

51

HEALTHY PATTERNS

We all develop coping habits to handle difficult situations, but not all of them are healthy for us or those around us. Even Abraham, a man of great faith, struggled with fear, presenting his wife Sarah as his sister, first in Egypt and later after Sodom and Gomorrah. His son Isaac repeated the same mistake.

The Bible reminds us that the patterns of one generation can affect the next, even to the third and fourth generation.

"Say you are my sister, so that I will be treated well
for your sake and my life will be spared because of you."
Genesis 12:13

"Abraham said of his wife Sarah, 'She is my sister.'
Then Abimelek king of Gerar sent for Sarah and took her."
Genesis 20:2

"You must not worship or serve any idol, because I, the Lord your
God, am a jealous God. If you hate me, I will punish your children,
and even your grandchildren and great-grandchildren. But I show
kindness to thousands who love me and obey my commands."
Exodus 20:5-6

"Yet he does not leave the guilty unpunished; he punishes the children and
their children for the sin of the parents to the third and fourth generation."
Exodus 34:7b

"For just as through the disobedience of the one man the
many were made sinners, so also through the obedience of
the one man the many will be made righteous."
Romans 5:19

*"Whoever has the Son has life, but whoever does not
have the Son of God does not have life."*
1 John 5:12

"As the Scripture says, 'Anyone who calls on the Lord will be saved.'"
Romans 10:13

*"Christ took away the curse the law put on us.
He changed places with us and put himself under that curse.
It is written in the Scriptures,
'Anyone whose body is displayed on a tree is cursed.'"*
Galatians 3:13

52

STEADY IN HIS STRENGTH

*"To God we are the aroma of Christ among those who
are saved and among those who are dying."*
2 Corinthians 2:15

God calls us to be steady and consistent, firm as a rock. He doesn't want us to be tossed about like waves in the sea, shifting from one direction to another, as James warns. Instead, He wants us to look into the mirror and see Christ in us, Christ crucified, Christ resurrected, the new creation.

He invites us to pick up our cross and bring it to His feet, passing from death into life through His resurrection power. We are to clothe ourselves in strength and faith, shaking off fear and uncertainty, and wear the royal garments of those redeemed by grace.

In our weakness, His grace is made perfect. When doubt and unbelief try to rise, His power shatters them. We walk in victory, confident in what He has done for us, humble, surrendered vessels crying out to be filled with His glory from on high.

*"Our faces, then, are not covered. We all show the Lord's glory,
and we are being changed to be like him. This change in us
brings ever greater glory, which comes from the Lord, who is the Spirit."*
2 Corinthians 3:18

THE DOOR IS OPEN

From the beginning of creation, God has spoken through His prophets, calling us to repentance, to be baptized, to walk by faith and not by sight, to live as conquerors, fearing nothing.

Now the hinges of heaven's door have burst open, and the veil has been torn. We have free access to the very presence of God, to His kingdom, His majesty, the Holy of Holies, where our spirits cry out, "Abba, Father!" and long to be transformed.

Here, in His presence, we taste the goodness of heaven and declare His covenant over our lives. We walk in Spirit and in truth, proclaiming liberty to the captives and freedom to the broken. The door is open. Enter in and receive all that He has promised.

"Rejoice and lean not on your own understanding
proclaimed the acceptable day of the Lord.
OH, give thanks to the Lord!
Call upon his name to make known his deeds among his people!
Sing to Him, sing psalms to Him:
Talk of all His wonderous works!
Glory in His holy name:
Let the hearts of those rejoice who seek the Lord!
Seek the Lord and His strength; Seek His face evermore!
Remember His marvelous works which He has done,
and the judgements of His mouth.
O seed of Abraham His servant,
You, children of Jacob.
His chosen ones!
He is the Lord our God His judgement is in all the earth.
He remembers His covenant forever,
God's Word stands firm through all generations,
the covenant He made with Abraham, confirmed with Isaac,
and established with Jacob as an everlasting promise to Israel.
His faithfulness never ends."
Psalm 105:1-10

LIVING IN PROPHETIC POWER

Prophecy is being fulfilled through the Word of God and through our very lives. Every detail reveals the prophetic power God longs to release in and through His people. This revelation comes to those who seek Jesus with their whole heart, those who desire to know nothing except Christ and Him crucified. They have laid down the flesh, taken up their cross, and chosen to follow Him fully.

Such people have emptied themselves so that the Holy Spirit can fill them completely. They live as servants of God, walking by faith and stepping into the prophetic destiny that was prepared for them long ago.

"For this reason, ever since I heard about your faith in the Lord Jesus and your love for all God's people, I have not stopped giving thanks for you, remembering you in my prayers. I keep asking that the God of our Lord Jesus Christ, the glorious Father, may give you the Spirit of wisdom and revelation, so that you may know him better. I pray that the eyes of your heart may be enlightened in order that you may know the hope to which he has called you, the riches of his glorious inheritance in his holy people, and his incomparably great power for us who believe. That power is the same as the mighty strength."
Ephesians 1:15-19

God has spoken a Word over your life—He has already ordered your steps. So step out in faith! As you press into Him, He becomes the wine press, drawing out His anointing within you. His presence will cover you, and His purpose will flow through you.

"The Son is the radiance of God's glory and the exact representation of his being, sustaining all things by his powerful word. After he had provided purification for sins, he sat down at the right hand of the Majesty in heaven."
Hebrews 1:3

WISE OR FOOLISH?

"At that time the kingdom of heaven will be like ten virgins who took their lamps and went out to meet the bridegroom. Five of them were foolish and five were wise. The foolish ones took their lamps but did not take any oil with them. The wise ones, however, took oil in jars along with their lamps. The bridegroom was a long time in coming, and they all became drowsy and fell asleep. At midnight the cry rang out: 'Here's the bridegroom! Come out to meet him!' Then all the virgins woke up and trimmed their lamps. The foolish ones said to the wise, 'Give us some of your oil; our lamps are going out.' 'No,' they replied, 'there may not be enough for both us and you. Instead, go to those who sell oil and buy some for yourselves.' But while they were on their way to buy the oil, the bridegroom arrived. The virgins who were ready went in with him to the wedding banquet. And the door was shut. Later the others also came. 'Lord, Lord,' they said, 'open the door for us!' But he replied, 'Truly I tell you, I don't know you.'"
Matthew 25:1-12

"Be dressed ready for service and keep your lamps burning."
Luke 12:35

In the story of the wise and foolish virgins, slumber overtook the unwise who slept. However, the wise remained alert and prepared for the bridegroom's arrival. We should not let worldly distractions make us like the unwise virgins. Instead, we must clear our minds of anything that diverts our focus from the coming of Christ.

We cast away anything that threatens our salvation and we bind every demonic spirit seeking to bring slumber upon us, causing us to lose the fragrance of Christ. We keep our lamps full and trimmed, the fire of the Holy Spirit burning, declaring the Word of God, and praying constantly for Christ's great return, in Jesus' name.

PRAY FOR THE HARVEST

"Yet at the same time many even among the leaders believed in him. But because of the Pharisees they would not openly acknowledge their faith for fear they would be put out of the synagogue; for they loved human praise more than praise from God. Then Jesus cried out, 'Whoever believes in me does not believe in me only, but in the one who sent me. The one who looks at me is seeing the one who sent me. I have come into the world as a light, so that no one who believes in me should stay in darkness. If anyone hears my words but does not keep them, I do not judge that person. For I did not come to judge the world, but to save the world. There is a judge for the one who rejects me and does not accept my words; the very words I have spoken will condemn them at the last day. For I did not speak on my own, but the Father who sent me commanded me to say all that I have spoken. I know that his command leads to eternal life. So whatever I say is just what the Father has told me to say.'"
John 12:42-50

The light of God wants to shine through you. These are dark times and the future feels uncertain. Just like in the days of old, many believe but won't confess Jesus as Lord. They're afraid of being rejected by the world. Yet Jesus is still calling out to them, pleading before His great and glorious return.

He's calling you to pray for the harvest, to share God's Word with clarity and truth. He wants you to *do something* with your faith; to walk in the power of God.

The Holy Spirit is ready, waiting for God's command, but you must also wait, listen, and be ready to go when you receive the word.

Holy Spirit, it's Your Word that judges us, not the world. Draw near to us, speak what You reveal, and we will go. Show us where to go and what to say. In Jesus' name.

57

DO YOU HEAR THE ROAR?

"But Lord, you are our father. We are like clay,
and you are the potter; your hands made us all."
Isaiah 64:8

We're meant to be confirmed by God, not by others. What God's Word says about you matters more than what people say. People will let you down, but don't let their actions cause you to compromise who you are in Christ. Let your mind be renewed so that God's Spirit can override your emotions and put to death the deeds of the flesh.

Inside you, the inner man is roaring to walk in spirit and in truth; to please God, not people. Your inner man is being shaped into a vessel for the Most High, stripped of self, layer by layer, becoming the person God created him to be.

58

DIVISION OR UNITY?

*"The eyes of the Lord search the whole earth in order to
strengthen those whose hearts are fully committed to him. What
a fool you have been! From now on you will be at war."*
2 Chronicles 16:9

Satan is always trying to enter the place of worship to cause disruption
and division. That's why God is raising up people with discerning spirits,
those who can recognize the enemy's schemes and sound the warning to
protect His people.

*"You are the children of your father, the Devil, and you want
to follow your father's desires. From the very beginning he was a
murderer and has never been on the side of truth, because there
is no truth in him. When he tells a lie, he is only doing what is
natural to him, because he is a liar and the father of all lies."*
John 8:44

From the very beginning, Satan has opposed God's truth and
stirred up rebellion. He is the one who started war in heaven.

But take heart. God is greater. The Spirit of discernment is not
given to create fear, but to equip and protect the Body of Christ. Those
who walk in the Spirit and stand firm in truth will always overcome the
enemy's plans.

*"Do you know where your fights and arguments come from? They come
from the selfish desires that war within you. You want things, but you do
not have them. So you are ready to kill and are jealous of other people, but
you still cannot get what you want. So you argue and fight. You do not get
what you want, because you do not ask God. Or when you ask, you do not
receive because the reason you ask is wrong. You want things so you can use
them for your own pleasures. So, you are not loyal to God! You should know*

*that loving the world is the same as hating God. Anyone who wants to be
a friend of the world becomes God's enemy. Do you think the Scripture
means nothing that says, 'The Spirit that God made to live in us wants
us for himself alone'? But God gives us even more grace, as the Scripture
says, 'God is against the proud, but he gives grace to the humble.'"*
James 4:1-6

DAY

59

GOD'S OATH

Romans 11:29 tells us the gifts and the callings of God are irrevocable.

Oh God, we come before you with open hearts, setting aside every burden that weighs us down. We choose to focus on the hope you've placed before us.

Your Word reminds us that you wanted to show your unchanging purpose to those who would inherit your promise. So you confirmed it with an oath, so that by two unchangeable things, and because it's impossible for you to lie, we can be deeply encouraged. We've run to you for safety, and we hold tightly to the hope you've given us.

> *"Now when people take an oath, they call on someone greater than themselves to hold them to it. And without any question that oath is binding. God also bound himself with an oath, so that those who received the promise could be perfectly sure that he would never change his mind. So God has given both his promise and his oath. These two things are unchangeable because it is impossible for God to lie. Therefore, we who have fled to him for refuge can have great confidence as we hold to the hope that lies before us. This hope is a strong and trustworthy anchor for our souls. It leads us through the curtain into God's inner sanctuary."*
> Hebrews 6:16-19

Lord Jesus, we come to you in prayer, asking for the riches of Your presence, the Christ within us. Though our earthly bodies are marked by sin, Your Spirit gives us life through righteousness. We declare that we are the righteousness of God in Christ Jesus. We are holy, redeemed, and bought at a great price to glorify You with our bodies, minds, and spirits. You have given us the mind of Christ. By Your resurrection power, You raised us to new life and seated us with You in heavenly places. Your Spirit confirms that we are Your children, and from deep within, our hearts cry out, "Abba, Father." Fill us with the riches of full assurance and understanding. Shape us into Your image. Reveal to us the mysteries of God the Father and Christ Jesus our Lord. Amen.

SPEAKING GOD'S WORD

"Finally, brethren, whatever things are true, whatever things are noble, whatever things are just, whatever things are pure, whatever things are lovely, whatever things are of good report, if there is any virtue and if there is anything praiseworthy—meditate on these things."
Philippians 4:8

What we think about carries great power. But let's go deeper. If we don't remove false beliefs and wrong perceptions, they can cloud and suppress the image of Christ within us. That's why it's so important to speak God's Word out loud.

When we begin to declare who God says we are and stop believing the lies spoken by others or whispered by the enemy, we open ourselves to transformation. We wait humbly, trusting the Holy Spirit to shape us more and more into the image of Christ.

"Search me, O God, and know my heart; try me, and know my anxieties, and see if there is any wicked way in me, and lead me in the way everlasting."
Psalm 139:23-24

"Therefore we do not lose heart. Even though our outward man is perishing, yet the inward man is being renewed day by day. For our light affliction, which is but for a moment, is working for us a far more exceeding and eternal weight of glory, while we do not look at the things which are seen, but at the things which are not seen. For the things which are seen are temporary, but the things which are not seen are eternal."
2 Corinthians 4:16-18

61

SHIFTS

When we call on God in the name of Jesus, things begin to shift because there is power in His name. When we pray with faith, we align ourselves with His will and invite His presence into our lives.

"And whatever you ask in My name, that I will do,
that the Father may be glorified in the Son.
If you ask anything in My name, I will do it."
John 14:13-14

Our actions reveal the depth of our faith. When we truly believe God's Word, Scripture tells us that the Holy Spirit will move on our behalf and fulfill what God has promised.

Faith isn't just what we say, it's what we live. And when we align our lives with God's truth, His Spirit works within us to bring that truth to life.

"When the Spirit of truth comes, he will guide you into all the truth.
For he will not speak on his own, but he will speak whatever he hears."
John 16:13

"If you believe, you will receive whatever you ask for in prayer."
Matthew 21:22

"So I tell you to believe that you have received the things
you ask for in prayer, and God will give them to you."
Mark 11:24

"This is the confidence we have in approaching God:
that if we ask anything according to his will, he hears us.
And if we know that he hears us—whatever we ask—we know
that we have what we asked of him."
1 John 5:14-15

We know that God is good, and that He never changes. He is the same yesterday, today, and forever. Every good and perfect gift comes from above, from the Father of heavenly lights, who remains constant and faithful, never shifting like shadows.

DECREE AND DECLARE

I speak opportunities to serve and bless God and others. I speak increase in my health, my finances, and every area of my life. I speak healing over my family, friends, and loved ones. I speak prosperity and peace, in Jesus' name!

"Do not confess the negative thoughts in your mind,
rather speak life to every situation around you."
Proverbs 30:32

"You will succeed in all you do, and light will shine on your path."
Job 22:28

OUR SUFFICIENCY IS FROM GOD.

In Judges 7, we read how Gideon started with an army of thirty-two thousand men, already outnumbered by the Midianites. But then God told him, "You have too many men." So Gideon sent home everyone who was afraid, and two-thirds of his army left. That brought him down to just ten thousand. But God said again, "There are still too many." Finally, the army was reduced to only three hundred men. The odds were impossible: a million to one. And here's the amazing part: God told Gideon to go into battle armed only with trumpets and clay pitchers. And with that small, faithful army, Israel won the victory!

Why did God do it like that? Because if Gideon had gone into battle with thirty-two thousand men and won, the Israelites might have thought they did it on their own, and God would've received only part of the credit. But God deserves all the glory. So when three hundred men defeated a massive army using nothing but trumpets and pitchers, there was no question who made it happen. God did.

Sometimes we pray for God to make things easier or to stack the odds in our favor. But maybe God wants the odds against us so we can see His power at work and experience a miracle only He could make happen.

Faith means trusting God even when the odds seem impossible. What looks hopeless to us is an opportunity for God to show His glory in a whole new way. Are you facing something that feels too big to handle on your own? That's exactly where God loves to show up, right in the middle of the impossible.

"We are not saying that we can do this work ourselves.
It is God who makes us able to do all that we do."
2 Corinthians 3:5

DAY

64

STANDING FIRM

When we pray in the Spirit, we stand against principalities and powers of darkness. We cast out demons, tear down strongholds, and release the light of God to bring freedom and victory into people's lives.

"For where two or three are gathered together in
My name, there am I in the midst of them."
Matthew 18:20

Here's an example of prayer and intercession found in Scripture:

"As long as Moses held up his arms, the Israelites won, but when he put his arms down, the Amalekites started winning. When Moses' arms grew tired, Aaron and Hur brought a stone for him to sit on, while they stood beside him and held up his arms, holding them steady until the sun went down. In this way Joshua totally defeated the Amalekites."
Exodus 17:12

Victory often comes through perseverance in prayer and through the strength of community. When one grows tired, others step in to lift them up. Together, we see God's power released and His people walk in victory. It is by the name of Jesus that the enemy was defeated, and in the name of Jesus, the enemy is defeated even now!

SILENCE

Sometimes we need to shut everything out, just like Jesus did. The Father longs to spend that quiet, personal time with us. It's in those moments alone with Him that we find the strength to do His will.

"Immediately Jesus made his disciples get into the boat and go before him to the other side while he sent the multitudes away. And when he had sent the multitudes away, he went up on the mountain by himself to pray. Now when evening came he was alone."
Matthew 14:22-23

Lord, forgive me for the times I haven't taken time to be alone with You. I repent and ask that You fill me with a spirit of worship. Help me remember that every moment I have is a gift from You, that I live and breathe only because of You. I owe You everything, Lord. Thank You for Your mercy and love. Amen.

66

EYES FIXED ON JESUS

We all want to feel valued and have the freedom to express who we are. Each of us was created for a purpose that others may not always see, but God sees it all. He knows everything. Before we even wake up, He's already planned our day, the surprises, the challenges, every detail. But how we respond is up to us.

Lord, help us in those valley moments when we face hard decisions. If something doesn't point to You, give us the wisdom to wait and not move without Your direction.

Holy Spirit, our counselor, comforter, and teacher, fill us with the same power You gave Peter when he asked Jesus to call him out onto the water. And above all, help us keep our eyes fixed on Jesus, no matter what things look like around us. Amen.

THE SACRIFICE

*"Then King David said to his officials, 'Don't you realize that a great
commander has fallen today in Israel? And even
though I am the anointed king,
these two sons of Zeruiah—Joab and Abishai—
are too strong for me to control.
So may the Lord repay these evil men for their evil deeds.'"*
2 Samuel 3:38-39

In God's kingdom, there are vessels of honor and vessels of dishonor,
but all of it ultimately works for His glory.

*"For all have sinned and fall short of the glory of God,
and all are justified freely by his grace through the
redemption that came by Christ Jesus."*
Romans 3:23-24

The power of sin ran its course until Christ came to conquer sin
and death once and for all, offering Himself as the ultimate, eternal
sacrifice.

DAY

68

STRATEGY

God has strategically placed you in certain situations or circumstances, even ones you may not like or understand. He's waiting for you to take the next step so He can move.

"Miriam and Aaron began to talk against Moses because of his Cushite wife, for he had married a Cushite. 'Has the Lord spoken only through Moses?' they asked. 'Hasn't he also spoken through us?' And the Lord heard this. (Now Moses was a very humble man, more humble than anyone else on the face of the earth.) At once the Lord said to Moses, Aaron and Miriam, 'Come out to the tent of meeting, all three of you.' So the three of them went out. Then the Lord came down in a pillar of cloud; he stood at the entrance to the tent and summoned Aaron and Miriam. When the two of them stepped forward, he said, 'Listen to my words: When there is a prophet among you, I, the Lord, reveal myself to them in visions, I speak to them in dreams. But this is not true of my servant Moses; he is faithful in all my house. With him I speak face to face, clearly and not in riddles; he sees the form of the Lord. Why then were you not afraid to speak against my servant Moses?' The anger of the Lord burned against them, and he left them. When the cloud lifted from above the tent, Miriam's skin was leprous—it became as white as snow. Aaron turned toward her and saw that she had a defiling skin disease, and he said to Moses, 'Please, my lord, I ask you not to hold against us the sin we have so foolishly committed. Do not let her be like a stillborn infant coming from its mother's womb with its flesh half eaten away.' So Moses cried out to the Lord, 'Please, God, heal her!' The Lord replied to Moses, 'If her father had spit in her face, would she not have been in disgrace for seven days? Confine her outside the camp for seven days; after that she can be brought back.' So Miriam was confined outside the camp for seven days, and the people did not move on till she was brought back."
Numbers 12:1-15

Lord, help us to leave our opinions out of what You are doing and to be humble like Moses. Teach us to be thankful for however You choose to use us. Forgive us for wanting more or trying to do more instead of simply serving You in the way You decide. Help us stay humble and willing, no matter what. Amen.

69

KNOWING GOD IS KNOWING HIS WILL

"This is the confidence we have in approaching God: that if we ask anything according to his will, he hears us. And if we know that he hears us—whatever we ask—we know that we have what we asked of him."
John 5:14-15

God is calling us to be persistent in His will. His Word is His will, and the Spirit is calling us to obey it. We must keep asking, seeking, and remaining consistent. An example of this kind of consistency is found in Scripture.

"Then, teaching them more about prayer, he used this story: 'Suppose you went to a friend's house at midnight, wanting to borrow three loaves of bread. You say to him, "A friend of mine has just arrived for a visit, and I have nothing for him to eat." And suppose he calls out from his bedroom, "Don't bother me. The door is locked for the night, and my family and I are all in bed. I can't help you." But I tell you this—though he won't do it for friendship's sake, if you keep knocking long enough, he will get up and give you whatever you need because of your shameless persistence. And so I tell you, keep on asking, and you will receive what you ask for. Keep on seeking, and you will find. Keep on knocking, and the door will be opened to you. [For everyone who asks, receives. Everyone who seeks, finds. And to everyone who knocks, the door will be opened.'"
Luke 11:5-10

"For God so loved the world, that he gave his only begotten Son, that whosoever believeth in him should not perish, but have everlasting life. For God sent not his Son into the world to condemn the world; but that the world through him might be saved."
John 3:16-17

70

MEDITATION

"While I meditated, the fire burned; then I spoke with my tongue."
Psalm 39:3

When we dive into God's Word and meditate on it, the Holy Spirit can give us a message, a testimony, or a word to speak. Just like with Jeremiah, it becomes like fire in our bones. We can't keep it to ourselves; we have to share it. But sometimes we hesitate. We tell ourselves we're not qualified, focusing on our weaknesses and flaws. We let those thoughts try to stop us.

But what did God say to Jeremiah?

"But the Lord said to me, 'Do not say, "I am only a youth"; for to all to whom I send you, you shall go, and whatever I command you, you shall speak. Be not afraid of them, for I am with you to deliver you,' says the Lord. Then the Lord put forth his hand and touched my mouth; and the Lord said to me, 'Behold, I have put my words in your mouth. See, I have set you this day over nations and over kingdoms, to pluck up and to break down, to destroy and to overthrow, to build and to plant.'"
Jeremiah 1:7-11

God has commissioned us to go and make disciples. When we fail to do that, it's like giving the gospel a black eye

DAY
71

SANCTIFIED, SEALED, AND CHOSEN

My willingness is revealed through my actions. If I won't sacrifice my own wants and desires to obey the Holy Spirit, I won't reap God's spiritual harvest or bear the fruit of the Spirit.

A relationship with Jesus produces victories, and through the Holy Spirit, these victories are displayed by God's power. Suffering is the antidote to obedience—Jesus obeyed unto death to do the will of His Father.

I must live like Jesus lived and be willing to die to myself, just as He died. This dying to self happens as I obey and allow the Potter to mold my brokenness into a sculpture for the Master's use.

How is this possible? I must remain in constant communication with the Father, trusting Him fully. Throughout God's Word, we see this pattern over and over again.

"Jesus said to them, 'Truly, truly, I say to you, the Son can do nothing of his own accord, but only what he sees the Father doing; for whatever he does, that the Son does likewise. For the Father loves the Son, and shows him all that he himself is doing; and greater works than these will he show him, that you may marvel.'"
John 5:18-20

"For I have not spoken on My own authority; but the Father who sent Me gave Me a command, what I should say and what I should speak."
John 12:49

"The power of sin was death and the law could only be a temporary solution until Jesus came to conquer it. Jesus said, 'Do not think that I have come to abolish the Law or the Prophets; I have not come to abolish them but to fulfill them. For truly I tell you, until heaven and earth

*disappear, not the smallest letter, not the least stroke of a pen, will by
any means disappear from the Law until everything is accomplished.'"*
Matthew 5:17–18

The Holy Spirit is accomplishing in us a far greater phenomenon
--He has made us competent as ministers of a new covenant—not of the
letter but of the Spirit; for the letter kills, but the Spirit gives life.

*"For all who rely on works of the law are under a curse; for
it is written, 'Cursed be everyone who does not abide by all
things written in the Book of the Law, and do them.'"*
Galatians 3:10

*"For whoever keeps the whole law but fails in one point has become
guilty of all of it.yet we know that a person is not justified by works of
the law but through faith in Jesus Christ, so we also have believed in
Christ Jesus, in order to be justified by faith in Christ and not by works
of the law, because by works of the law no one will be justified."*
Galatians 2:15-16

*"It is the Spirit that gives life. The flesh doesn't give life.
The words I told you are spirit, and they give life."*
John 6:63

*"He is the Holy Spirit, who leads into all truth. The world cannot receive
him, because it isn't looking for him and doesn't recognize him. But you
know him, because he lives with you now and later will be in you."*
John 14:17

*"And you also were included in Christ when you heard the message
of truth, the gospel of your salvation. When you believed, you
were marked in him with a seal, the promised Holy Spirit, who
is a deposit guaranteeing our inheritance until the redemption of
those who are God's possession—to the praise of his glory."*
Ephesians 1:13-14

DAY
72
ACTIONS

*"Now this is our boast: Our conscience testifies that we have
conducted ourselves in the world, and especially in our relations
with you, with integrity and godly sincerity. We have done
so, relying not on worldly wisdom but on God's grace."*
2 Corinthians 1:12

Have you ever heard the saying, *"Actions speak louder than words,"* or
"Sticks and stones may break my bones, but words will never hurt me"?

The truth is, what I say and do to myself and to others can affect
everything. But how I respond reveals my love for God. At the end of
the day, I can only be responsible for my own words and actions.

So I have to ask myself: am I acting according to the flesh or
according to the Spirit? Do I see things through faith, or do I see them
through my own carnal human nature?

That question made me take a hard look at myself. When I studied
the Greek and Hebrew meaning of the word *carnal*, I found something
powerful. The Thayer's Greek Lexicon defines *sarkikos (carnal)* as
"governed by mere human nature, not by the Spirit of God."

That hit me deeply. It reminded me that even Jesus, who was fully
God and fully man, faced the tension of human weakness. Yet He never
gave in. He lived by the Spirit perfectly, showing us how to overcome
our flesh through obedience and faith.

*"…who, in the days of His flesh, when He had offered up prayers and
supplications, with vehement cries and tears to Him who was able to save
Him from death, and was heard because of His godly fear, though He
was a Son, yet He learned obedience by the things which He suffered."*
Hebrews 5:7-8

We must always remember *sarkikos-* pertaining to the flesh; bodily;
temporal. We must press forward to eternal things.

"We have this treasure from God, but we are like clay jars that hold the treasure. This shows that the great power is from God, not from us. We have troubles all around us, but we are not defeated. We do not know what to do, but we do not give up the hope of living. We are persecuted, but God does not leave us. We are hurt sometimes, but we are not destroyed. We carry the death of Jesus in our own bodies so that the life of Jesus can also be seen in our bodies. We are alive, but for Jesus we are always in danger of death so that the life of Jesus can be seen in our bodies that die. So death is working in us, but life is working in you. It is written in the Scriptures, 'I believed, so I spoke.' Our faith is like this, too. We believe, and so we speak. [God raised the Lord Jesus from the dead, and we know that God will also raise us with Jesus. God will bring us together with you, and we will stand before him. All these things are for you. And so the grace of God that is being given to more and more people will bring increasing thanks to God for his glory. So we do not give up. Our physical body is becoming older and weaker, but our spirit inside us is made new every day. We have small troubles for a while now, but they are helping us gain an eternal glory that is much greater than the troubles. We set our eyes not on what we see but on what we cannot see. What we see will last only a short time, but what we cannot see will last forever."

2 Corinthians 4:7-18

TREATMENT OF OTHERS

"Some time later King Xerxes promoted Haman son of Hammedatha the Agagite over all the other nobles, making him the most powerful official in the empire. All the king's officials would bow down before Haman to show him respect whenever he passed by, for so the king had commanded. But Mordecai refused to bow down or show him respect.

"Then the palace officials at the king's gate asked Mordecai, 'Why are you disobeying the king's command?' They spoke to him day after day, but still he refused to comply with the order. So they spoke to Haman about this to see if he would tolerate Mordecai's conduct, since Mordecai had told them he was a Jew. When Haman saw that Mordecai would not bow down or show him respect, he was filled with rage. He had learned of Mordecai's nationality, so he decided it was not enough to lay hands on Mordecai alone. Instead, he looked for a way to destroy all the Jews throughout the entire empire of Xerxes. So in the month of April, during the twelfth year of King Xerxes' reign, lots were cast in Haman's presence (the lots were called purim) to determine the best day and month to take action. And the day selected was March 7, nearly a year later. Then Haman approached King Xerxes and said, 'There is a certain race of people scattered through all the provinces of your empire who keep themselves separate from everyone else. Their laws are different from those of any other people, and they refuse to obey the laws of the king. So it is not in the king's interest to let them live. If it please the king, issue a decree that they be destroyed, and I will give 10,000 large sacks of silver to the government administrators to be deposited in the royal treasury.' The king agreed, confirming his decision by removing his signet ring from his finger and giving it to Haman son of Hammedatha the Agagite, the enemy of the Jews. The king said, 'The money and the people are both yours to do with as you see fit.'"

Esther 3:1-10

Many times, I've chosen the path of faith for what I believed in, even when others couldn't understand. I saw something they couldn't see. I felt something they couldn't feel.

"My dear friends, many false prophets have gone out into the world. So do not believe every spirit, but test the spirits to see if they are from God."
1 John 4:1

How others treat you reveals the spirit they carry. You can see it in what they do and don't do, what they say and don't say. Altogether, that shows us there are three kinds of people.

1. People who make things happen.
2. People who watch things happen.
3. People who don't know what happened.

Mordecai was a person of action and conviction. People of faith have always stood out, often been misunderstood, labeled, taken advantage of, even persecuted or killed. Many were called crazy or too radical, yet throughout the Bible, it's those very people who took a stand and brought real change.

Are you willing to be that kind of person today? Someone who refuses to just "go along to get along"? Someone who would rather die standing for truth than live in a world full of injustice?

Because obeying God will always matter more than pleasing people.

And when you look at Mordecai's story, you can see that when one person's vision and passion for God and His people ignite, transformation follows.

"That night the king had trouble sleeping, so he ordered an attendant to bring the book of the history of his reign so it could be read to him. In those records he discovered an account of how Mordecai had exposed the plot of Bigthana and Teresh, two of the eunuchs who guarded the door to the king's private quarters. They had plotted to assassinate King Xerxes. 'What reward or recognition did we ever give Mordecai for this?' the king asked. His attendants replied, 'Nothing has been done for him.' 'Who is that in the outer court?' the king inquired. As it happened, Haman had just

*arrived in the outer court of the palace to ask the king to impale Mordecai
on the pole he had prepared. So the attendants replied to the king, 'Haman
is out in the court.' 'Bring him in,' the king ordered. So Haman came in,
and the king said, 'What should I do to honor a man who truly pleases
me?' Haman thought to himself, 'Whom would the king wish to honor
more than me?' So he replied, 'If the king wishes to honor someone, he
should bring out one of the king's own royal robes, as well as a horse that
the king himself has ridden—one with a royal emblem on its head. Let the
robes and the horse be handed over to one of the king's most noble officials.
And let him see that the man whom the king wishes to honor is dressed in
the king's robes and led through the city square on the king's horse. Have
the official shout as they go, "This is what the king does for someone he
wishes to honor!" 'Excellent!' the king said to Haman. 'Quick! Take the
robes and my horse, and do just as you have said for Mordecai the Jew,
who sits at the gate of the palace. Leave out nothing you have suggested!'*

*"So Haman took the robes and put them on Mordecai, placed him on
the king's own horse, and led him through the city square, shouting,
'This is what the king does for someone he wishes to honor!' Afterward
Mordecai returned to the palace gate, but Haman hurried home
dejected and completely humiliated. When Haman told his wife,
Zeresh, and all his friends what had happened, his wise advisers
and his wife said, 'Since Mordecai—this man who has humiliated
you—is of Jewish birth, you will never succeed in your plans.'"*
Esther 6:1-13

74

FIRE

Everybody wants fire, but no one wants to go through the fire. Shadrach, Meshach, and Abednego walked willingly into the fiery furnace. They were met by opposition to bow down, to reject God, and to renounce God Almighty.

As I was listening to someone share their experience, strength, and hope, they said they used to walk around the fire but learned if they went through it, God revealed what was needed to help them be victorious.

Then I remembered 1 Peter 4:12-19:

"Dear friends, don't be surprised at the fiery trials you are going through, as if something strange were happening to you. Instead, be very glad—for these trials make you partners with Christ in his suffering, so that you will have the wonderful joy of seeing his glory when it is revealed to all the world."

If you are insulted because you bear the name of Christ, you will be blessed, for the glorious Spirit of God rests upon you. If you suffer, however, it must not be for murder, stealing, making trouble, or prying into other people's affairs. But it is no shame to suffer for being a Christian. Praise God for the privilege of being called by his name! For the time has come for judgment, and it must begin with God's household. And if judgment begins with us, what terrible fate awaits those who have never obeyed God's Good News? And also, "If the righteous are barely saved, what will happen to godless sinners?" So if you are suffering in a manner that pleases God, keep on doing what is right, and trust your lives to the God who created you, for he will never fail you.

Then I came across this prayer to strengthen me on my road of recovery.

Blessed Holy Spirit, I pray that your presence would overshadow me. That you would bring your fire into my life. Burn in me such a passion for you that I would not be able to contain it. Let that fire be stoked and continue to burn the rest of my days. And let those who are around me experience your presence and fire. Lord, let your fire cleanse me and bring light to wherever I go. Let me be soft hearted and courageous toward its ability to purify me! Teach me Holy Spirit! Draw me close to you! Let my life be a flame before you. Help me to become a living sacrifice before you. I love you Holy Spirit and thank you for your fire. Thank you, that you are faithful to do this work within me.

In the mighty name of Jesus, amen and amen!

DAY

75

PART FLESH, PART SPIRIT

Born into this world in an earthly vessel, part Spirit and part flesh, predestined to live forever, created for greatness. Victory awaits this tiresome journey, always watching, always striving, always hoping, always dying, always praying, always believing, always knocking, always seeking, always finding strength to make it one more day.

"Therefore, we do not lose heart. Though our outer self is wasting away, yet our inner self is being renewed day by day. For our light and momentary affliction is producing for us an eternal glory that is far beyond comparison. So we fix our eyes not on what is seen, but on what is unseen. For what is seen is temporary, but what is unseen is eternal."
2 Corinthians 4:16-18

"Now we know that if the earthly tent we live in is dismantled, we have a building from God, an eternal house in heaven, not built by human hands. For in this tent we groan, longing to be clothed with our heavenly dwelling, because when we are clothed, we will not be found naked. So while we are in this tent, we groan under our burdens, because we do not wish to be unclothed but clothed, so that our mortality may be swallowed up by life. And God has prepared us for this very purpose and has given us the Spirit as a pledge of what is to come."
2 Corinthians 5:1-5

HUNGER AND THIRST

The desert is hot. It zaps you, dehydrating what your body needs to function physically, creating thirst and hunger.

The world has elements that Satan uses to draw you away from the things of God.

When Jesus was lead out to the wilderness by the Holy Spirit, He fasted 40 days and 40 nights before being tempted.

Sometimes God allows us to be tested to reveal whether our faith is genuine. He removes us from what is comfortable and takes us to hostile places that are uncomfortable that seem to have no way out.

But notice how Jesus was never alone. He had the Comforter and so do we.

Remember, no matter what it looks or seems like, the Holy Spirit has gone before you. There is no temptation or trial that will overcome you.

"I have said these things to you, that in me you may
have peace. In the world you will have tribulation.
But take heart; I have overcome the world."
1 John 4:4 ESV

77

HEART OF WORSHIP

There is a powerful story found in 2 Kings chapters 18 and 19. When Hezekiah became king, he boldly removed the high places, shattered the sacred pillars, cut down the wooden images, and destroyed the bronze serpent that Moses had made because the people had begun to worship it.

Hezekiah trusted in the Lord, the God of Israel, more than any king of Judah before or after him. He remained faithful, never turning away from God's commands, and carefully following all that the Lord had instructed through Moses. Because of this, the Lord was with him, and Hezekiah prospered wherever he went. He even stood up against the king of Assyria, refusing to submit.

However, the king of Assyria eventually led Israel into exile, scattering them across Halah, the Habor River of Gozan, and the cities of the Medes. This happened because they had turned away from God, breaking His covenant and ignoring the commands given through Moses.

The Assyrian king went on to capture many cities of Judah, surrounding and trapping them. Despite Hezekiah's earlier resistance, Judah ultimately fell into despair, just as the Scriptures recount.

"I have offended in denying the usual tribute,
and am ready to make satisfaction as shall be demanded."
2 Kings 18:14

At that time, Hezekiah stripped the gold from the doors at the temple of the Lord and from the pillars, which Hezekiah, king of Judah, had overlaid and he then gave the gold to the king of Assyria.

Satan's tactic is the offer you freedom. To sow seeds of doubt into your life. Compromise, conversation, and bargaining is the strategy he uses. Just as Satan sends messengers to divide, conquer, and instill fear, so did the king of Assyria.

What is this confidence in which you trust? You speak of strategy and strength, but they are empty words. In whom do you place your trust, that you dare to rebel against me?

"Do not listen to Hezekiah. This is what the king of Assyria says: Make peace with me and come out to me. Then each of you will eat fruit from your own vine and fig tree and drink water from your own cistern, until I come and take you to a land like your own, a land of grain and new wine, a land of bread and vineyards, a land of olive trees and honey. Choose life and not death!

"Do not listen to Hezekiah, for he is misleading you when he says, 'The Lord will deliver us.' Has the god of any nation ever delivered his land from the hand of the king of Assyria? Where are the gods of Hamath and Arpad? Where are the gods of Sepharvaim, Hena and Ivvah? Have they rescued Samaria from my hand? Who of all the gods of these countries has been able to save his land from me? How then can the Lord deliver Jerusalem from my hand?"

But the people remained silent and said nothing in reply, because the king had commanded, "Do not answer him."
Kings 18:31-36

Living out our faith doesn't always require us to respond or explain, but it does require us to stand firm. Like King Hezekiah and the tribe of Judah, we must choose to trust in the promises of God. The battle was never ours to win alone, it belonged to the Lord.

"Be strong and brave. Don't be afraid or worried because of the king of Assyria or his large army. There is a greater power with us than with him. He only has men, but we have the Lord our God to help us and to fight our battles."
2 Chronicles 32:7-8

A PRAYER FOR DELIVERANCE

"Lord, God of Israel, whose throne is between the gold creatures with wings, only you are God of all the kingdoms of the earth. You made the heavens and the earth. Hear, Lord, and listen. Open your eyes, Lord, and see. Listen to the words Sennacherib has said to insult the living God. It is true, Lord, that the kings of Assyria have destroyed these countries and their lands. They have thrown the gods of these nations into the fire, but they were only wood and rock statues that people made. So the kings have destroyed them. 19 Now, Lord our God, save us from the king's power so that all the kingdoms of the earth will know that you, Lord, are the only God."
2 Kings 19:15-19

"That night the angel of the Lord went out and put to death a hundred and eighty-five thousand in the Assyrian camp. When the people got up the next morning, there were all the dead bodies! So Sennacherib king of Assyria broke camp and withdrew. He returned to Nineveh and stayed there. One day, while he was worshiping in the temple of his god Nisrok, his sons Adrammelek and Sharezer killed him with the sword, and they escaped to the land of Ararat. And Esarhaddon his son succeeded him as king."
2 Kings 19:35-37

DAY

78

WORD MANIFEST

2 Corinthians 5:7 tells us, *"For we walk by faith, not by sight."* And Proverbs 18:21 reminds us, *"Death and life are in the power of the tongue, and those who love it will eat its fruit."*

Through faith, there is power. Jesus demonstrated this when He spoke to the fig tree, and it withered (Mark 11:12–14; 21–24). Though it wasn't the season for figs, Jesus spoke a word, and the tree died from the roots. The next day, the disciples saw the result of His spoken faith. Jesus then said, *"Have faith in God… if anyone says to this mountain, 'Go, throw yourself into the sea,' and does not doubt in their heart but believes, it will be done."*

Jesus also showed us the power of faith-filled words when He raised Lazarus from the dead (John 11:38–44). Even when death seemed final, Jesus thanked the Father, spoke with authority, and called Lazarus out of the grave. And Lazarus came forth. Then Jesus said, *"Take off the grave clothes and let him go."*

That command still speaks to us today. Jesus is calling us to remove whatever is binding our faith, to take off the grave clothes of fear, doubt, unbelief, and the patterns of this world. He is calling us to act on what we hear in the Spirit, to loose and bind according to the Word of God, and to allow His Word to manifest through obedient faith.

We are called:

To speak to circumstances,
To cry out in the name of Jesus, and
To believe that God's Word will come to pass when we speak by faith.

DAY

79

THE SOIL OF THE PASTURE

As sheep in God's pasture, we must be careful what we are feeding on. We are called to eat what nourishes us—not to gorge ourselves on the wildness of the flesh or consume false doctrine scattered throughout the field. What we eat spiritually determines our growth and our fruit.

In the field, not everything that grows is good. There are tares among the wheat. The cares of this world and the wiles of the devil creep in quietly. Scripture warns us that the enemy lurks, seeking whom he may devour. When we are not discerning, the cares of this life begin to poison the crop, weakening the integrity of God's Word in our hearts.

There are two primary spiritual dangers that threaten the believer's walk:

Internal Corruption — the Flesh. The lust of the flesh and the lust of the eyes represent the inward pull toward sin, self-gratification, and worldly desire. When we fail to "eat properly," we spiritually indulge in what feels good instead of what is good. This weakens our spirit and dulls our discernment.

External Corruption — False Doctrine and the World. False doctrine and worldly influences act like tares, resembling truth, yet slowly corrupting it. They distort the Word, compromise holiness, and weaken obedience.

At the root of both dangers lies pride, a focus on self, status, and earthly gain. It crowds out humility, dependence on God, and submission to His Word.

The Parable of the Sower and the Cares of the World reveal how the condition of the heart determines the fruitfulness of the Word.

The Thorny Ground — The Crowded Heart. This soil represents believers who receive the Word but allow it to be crowded out. The cares of this life: worry, anxiety, fear about the future. The deceitfulness of wealth and pleasures of life: the pursuit of comfort, success, recognition, and status. The Word begins to grow, but it is choked. Not because of unbelief, but because God's Word is no longer first. Competing desires overtake spiritual priority, and fruitfulness is lost.

The Good Soil — The Receptive Heart. Good soil hears the Word, holds fast to it with an honest and good heart, and bears fruit with patience and perseverance (Luke 8:15). This soil survives: the pressure of affliction, the enemy's attempts to steal the Word, and the choking effect of worldly cares. The key is submission. Continually surrendering pride, worry, and desire to the authority of God's Word.

The Call to Discernment. God is calling His sheep to discern the soil of their own hearts. To remove the tares. To guard what we consume. To feed on truth alone. Because what grows in the pasture determines what grows in us. And only good soil produces lasting fruit.

OUR PATH

"Therefore, since we are surrounded by such a great cloud of witnesses, let us throw off everything that hinders and the sin that so easily entangles. And let us run with perseverance the race marked out for us."
Hebrews 12:1

God has placed a unique path before us. That path may include moments of failure, just as Peter's did when he denied Christ three times. Failure does not cancel God's calling. When we repent and return to Him, He restores us and continues His work in our lives.

"'Simon, Simon, behold, Satan demanded to have you, that he might sift you like wheat, but I have prayed for you that your faith may not fail. And when you have turned again, strengthen your brothers.' Peter said to him, 'Lord, I am ready to go with you both to prison and to death.' Jesus said, 'I tell you, Peter, the rooster will not crow this day, until you deny three times that you know me.'"
Luke 22:31-34

God's ultimate purpose is that we know Him. Out of a personal relationship with Him, our lives are transformed and shaped into what He has called us to do.

After Jesus rose from the dead, Scripture tells us that He breathed on the disciples, and they received the empowerment of the Holy Spirit. Later, in John 21:15–17, Jesus personally restored Peter. Three times He asks, "Do you love Me?"

This moment was not just restoration, it was confirmation. Jesus reaffirmed Peter's calling to strengthen and shepherd others.

"You are Peter, and on this rock I will build My church, and the gates of Hades shall not prevail against it."
Matthew 16:18

Peter's life reflects God's redemptive process. He went from fisherman, to failure, to restoration, and ultimately leading the believers with power and faith.

Peter's story reminds us that failure is not final. God's grace restores, His Spirit empowers, and His calling remains greater than our mistakes.

I was born in Kansas City, Kansas, the youngest boy of three sisters. As a kid, I poured myself into sports, baseball, basketball, and BMX racing.

My first encounter with church came from a simple motivation: I wanted to win a Bible. After attending for sixteen weeks, I earned that pure white Bible and memorized my very first scripture, Isaiah 1:18:

"'Come now, and let us reason together,' says the Lord.
'Though your sins are like scarlet, they shall be as white as snow;
though they are red like crimson, they shall be as wool.'"

I didn't understand it then, but that verse would one day become the foundation of my story.

As I think back, I see all the false identities I tried to live up to coming from my environment, my insecurities, and my brokenness. Today, I stand confident in who I am in Christ. My past no longer defines me. I am a new creation, and I refuse to allow the enemy to chain me to who I used to be.

Growing up, drugs and alcohol surrounded me, and by eighteen, my choices led me into serious trouble. I was sentenced to prison, and I felt shattered. But God has a way of taking broken pieces and creating something beautiful.

In 1989, at twenty-two years old and still behind bars, I met a man whose peace and joy were unlike anything I had ever seen. Through him, I surrendered my life to Jesus and was born again. The transformation inside me was immediate, even if my circumstances were not. I didn't understand that forgiveness doesn't erase consequences. I wanted out of prison; I even tried to escape. It took time for me to learn that God opens doors in His timing, not mine.

After completing my sentence, I walked out of those prison gates filled with the Holy Spirit and on fire for Jesus. This book is a testimony of that journey, from brokenness to redemption, from captivity to freedom, from who I once was to who I am now in Christ.

Today I spend my time ministering to those people walking through the same struggles I once faced: addiction, homelessness, and incarceration. God uses my story to show them His love.